"Hope: An Anchor of the Soul"
(Hebrews 6:19)

Ruth Ann Howell

© 2011 By Ruth Ann Howell
All Rights Reserved

No part of this publication shall be reproduced by any means nor stored in a retrieval system of any kind without the prior written consent of Ruth Ann Howell.

Edited by
Kevin Patrick Dillon
Edward B. Garner, Jr.

Cover Design and Formatting:
Clayton Mitchell

Revised June, 2014

Blessed Assurance can be ordered by contacting:
Ruth Ann Howell
P.O. Box 517
4628 Spinnaker Way
Orange Beach, Alabama 36561
1-251-980-1414

All scripture quotes, questions, and answers, unless otherwise noted, are taken from the King James Version of the Bible.

ISBN: 978-0-615-59956-4

Printed in the United States of America
by Lambert Book House
Florence, Alabama 35630

A MESSAGE FROM THE AUTHOR

I have studied the scriptures for many years and countless hours. I have searched for answers concerning my own personal salvation. I wanted assurance and confidence that I was living in such a way that I could spend eternity with my heavenly Father and with Jesus Christ my Savior. I have finally found the answers to all my questions, doubts, and insecurities. I can say this to you without doubt or reservation. My deep study and search for answers and my journey in this endeavor has indeed been a great blessing and joy to me. To spend time in the book and to digest God's word is so nourishing and fulfilling that I wonder why we so often neglect the study of God's word.

I have wanted this book to become a reality and to be a part of my legacy. Before I depart this world for a better place, I wanted to leave a record of my journey and of my diligent and long search for answers concerning my own personal salvation. I wanted to share my struggle to KNOW FOR CERTAIN THAT I AM SAVED!!! I also wanted to know how I could acquire "peace that passes understanding" (Philippians 4:7). Perhaps this could be an encouragement for others to STAND IN GOD'S GRACE (1 Peter 5:12), to continue to walk in the light (1 John 1:7), to keep-on-keeping-on, and to never give up. I have finally realized that SALVATION IF NOT A "MATTER OF PERFECTION", "IT IS A MATTER OF BEING FAITHFUL UNTO DEATH" (Revelation 2:10). "When I realized this eye-opener", it was a tremendous shock to me but it was a "matter of great joy". Why? Because this is something that I know I can do and YOU CAN TOO! ! !

To those who study the scriptures in this book, to those who seek answers to questions concerning salvation, I leave this message to you: I hope and pray that the words in this book will point you to the scriptures that will encourage you to stay the course, to go forth and teach the alien sinner who has no hope without contacting the blood of Christ in baptism. I also hope that these words will enable you to realize the great value and immense measure of happiness in God's gift of salvation, and I look forward to seeing you on the other side. . . heaven.

R. A. Howell

FOREWORD

The 1960's marked an era in the history of the Church of Christ when many gospel preachers delivered terrifying, fiery sermons on the judgment and hell. Born in 1940, Ruth Ann Howell was surrounded by this stressful environment where "thou shalt not" was the normal lesson topic and the "blessings in Christ" were largely omitted.

Ruth Ann didn't remember many sermons about God's grace, mercy, and love. In fact, she thought these to be denominational concepts! The sermons she heard on hell-fire and damnation so frightened her that she dared not miss a church service. She was afraid of God and hell and found no peace, joy, or contentment in her religion.

Baptized at the age of thirteen, Ruth Ann took her religion seriously. She fervently desired to go to heaven. But even into her twenties and thirties, she still felt an extreme fear of hell. No matter how hard she tried to be faithful and good, she feared she would fail and be lost. She expected to stub her toe and curse without having enough time to ask forgiveness. Her concept of God was of a vengeful ogre who would delight in jerking her up and flinging her into the devil's hell.

Ruth Ann had not been told of God's mercy and longsuffering. His grace was unknown to her. She continued to attend all Bible class programs, but Ruth was not taught how to apply God's truths to her life.

When Ruth Ann finally discovered that God was indeed a God of love, that He wanted her to go to heaven, and that He was genuinely concerned about her, she began to see a noticeable, dramatic change in her life. For the first time, Ruth Ann felt the scope of God's love.

Her experience has instilled within her the desire to share the assurance of her salvation with everyone she can reach. Ruth has taught ladies classes using the material in this book, and her students encouraged her to write down the ideas she taught them so they could share with others. The book is titled <u>'Blessed Assurance'</u> because that is what the knowledge of the love of God is to her.

Join Ruth Ann in discovering the pure pleasure of possessing salvation and finding the assurance that "perfect love casts out fear."

Kevin Dillon

My knowledge and acquaintance with David and Ruth Ann Howell goes back more than twenty-five years. This Christian couple through their years together have loved God supremely, respected the Bible, sought first the Kingdom, longed for the salvation of the lost, and lived daily in anticipation of Heaven. This book dealing with Christian assurance is the fruit of Ruth Ann's thoughts over the last several years. I am very happy to introduce her and to commend her writing to your study and everlasting benefit.

We all know that there is so much undeserved security in the religious world. Many feel that they are right with God when the divine record would say otherwise. Many say peace when there is no peace. Also, there is so much unjustified doubt among faithful saints of God. So many do not enjoy the journey and fail to know the unsurpassed peace that is truly to be had in the right relationship with God. Think of the aged children of God who have lived faithfully but have fear of death and have little or no confidence facing judgment. This book will lead you to a greater peace and more appreciation for the blessed assurance in the passages of God's word.

The Bible often refers to the joy of salvation and the full, unspeakable joy that is ours in Christ. I know that Ruth Ann will feel that all her efforts were well spent if just one saint is encouraged; yet, all who digest this book will be blessed immensely. In reading the book, I thought of such words as refreshing, reviving, and renewing. No doubt, many will be inspired to press forward and others will be challenged to try again.

Optimism centered in God has always been subject to criticism by unbelievers and Ruth Ann's optimism centered in God may be criticized, even by brethren, but all will be challenged to inventory their relationship with God which has to bring blessings. There is a big difference between pride and blessed assurance that the Lord makes available for the faithful. Pride condemns but assurance is a spiritual blessing enjoyed in Christ.

The style of this book is directed toward both brevity and clarity. One can be benefited greatly by a study of this book in a short amount of time. The book is appropriate for Bible Class material. Thoughtful questions and exercises are provided at the end of each chapter.

May our wonderful Lord bless this book toward only well, both in this world and the world to come.

Vance Hutton

Friends of Ruth Ann Howell have always regarded her as a person with high energy and zeal. Those traits have motivated her to bring to fruition this book that deals with a concept she has nourished for quite some time.

Many Christians can recall hearing preachers in years past who underscored obedience and a sense of continuing rigid duty in a tone that caused heavy burdens to people with sensitive emotional thresholds. Those ministers were usually highly respected because of the deep concern they had for the lost, and probably were not aware of the casualties left in the wake of their preaching. They were trying to reach people who were hardened in sinful lifestyles without realizing that some of the best people in their audiences were deciding to "give up" because they did not feel they could ever "measure up." Such tones were not conveyed everywhere but it was not good that they were presented without a loving balance in content anywhere.

Ruth Ann does not minimize the necessity of obedience and continuing faithfulness to God in order for us to be saved, but she does spotlight the beauty of hope that understanding God's Amazing Grace gives to us. The Gospel teaches us that "no one has to stay the way he is." God's grace is available for those in the pew as well as for those in the gutter. The "whole counsel of God" involves balance in teaching ''the truth in love," as we share the message of God's grace and the continuing power of the saving blood of Jesus Christ to those in both venues.

Jack Wilhelm

I began helping Ruth Ann with her book in 2009. Before I began, my prayer was that God would help me to become a stronger Christian and a better example to others. In order to be that person, I needed encouragement. By helping Ruth Ann, God began helping me. I wanted so much to know that when I am gone from this earth, that I could know that I would see my loved ones again someday. My husband had not attended church much and had no need for religion in his life, but within the last year he has renewed his faith and has been studying the word. What a blessing! My prayer is to encourage those around me in the assurance of their salvation and they might have peace in this.

This book is simple, but full of information that can be used to renew your faith, open your eyes and help you to become a better Christian. This one thing I know about Ruth Ann is that she truly desires to teach others, and that she wants everyone to reach heaven. She has great knowledge, and enjoys sharing what she knows. She and I hope that this book will help and encourage others as much as it has me.

Donna Reedy

Motivation comes in many ways and forms. Toward obedience to God's will, there are two important ones. The Bible says, "Behold therefore the goodness and severity of God: on them which fell severity; but toward thee, goodness, if thou continue in his goodness: otherwise thou also shalt be cut off' (Romans 11:22). Paul, the inspired penman of this verse, preached the whole counsel of God (ct. Acts 20:27). Unfortunately, some today do not. There are preachers who tell of God's grace, mercy, and kindness while omitting the severity of God. A recent poll revealed that sixty-nine percent of the pulpits across the nation do not believe there is a hell (Northwestern University School of Education). Others seem to want to scare us into obedience without the pull of God's love. Ruth Ann Howell seems to have grown up under the latter type of the two, and that left her wanting. She found what she needed, however, in God's word, the Bible.

Though I am very nearly the same age as she, my experience was different from Sister Howell's. After hearing the gospel preached for many years, I became a Christian in 1962. I grew up during the same time as Ruth Ann listening to the preaching of J. Walker Whittle and Porter King, both of Freed-Hardeman University. Their preaching was balanced. I obeyed the gospel of Christ during a gospel meeting in which Guy N. Woods was the preacher. He, too, was balanced. And Ira North was influential throughout the brotherhood. He wrote the book on balance (see Balance a Tried & Tested Formula for Church Growth; Gospel Advocate, 1983). In a Christian Chronicle article of 2009, Bobby Ross, Jr. reported that Mack Lyon's research "concluded that Churches of Christ experienced a steady upward membership trend in the post-World War II era." Lyon of In Search of the Lord's Way, an evangelistic television program based in Edmond, Oklahoma, said, " ... the emphasis was on leading souls to Christ for salvation, Nowadays, it is on "church growth." Two gospel preachers who had something to do with that "steady upward membership trend" were Willie Bradfield and Franklin Camp.

The most dynamic and energetic preacher I heard in my youth was W. A. Bradfield. I still remember his walking up, and down the single isle of the small church building, yelling, "No hope! No hope!" as he labored to move people to obedience. I have a book of Bradfield's lessons in which he recorded sixty sermon outlines. Of those sixty, about one dozen deal with punishment, condemnation, and hell as the results of disobedience. The rest are discussions of "Christ and the Church," "From Paradise to Paradise," "Heaven and Who Is Going There," "Marriage and the Home," "New Testament Worship," and such. Bradfield began preaching the gospel in 1945 and continued through the 1960s. He was from West Tennessee where I was reared, but he held several meetings in Alabama and saw 106 responses in Jasper, 114 in Huntsville, and 105 in Hamilton during some of those efforts. Franklin Camp was an Alabama preacher who published a book of sermons called Old Truths in New Robes in 1970. Of the fifty sermons in that book, perhaps about a half dozen are on the negative side. The others' include messages like: "Abundant Living," "A False Conception of God," Grow in Grace," "The Bible and Young People," and "Making Christianity Attractive."

Young minds and hearts are impressionable. We preachers do not know and appreciate what the youngest of our listeners hear and remember. In the past sixteen years that I have preached for the Ninth Avenue Church of Christ in Haleyville, Alabama, my lessons have been particularly, specifically, or exclusively on hell, probably, less than one dozen times. That is out of well over 1,000 sermons! I'm thinking that is not nearly enough; yet, every time I preached one of those sermons, I had a parent come to me to say, "My son (or daughter) was really affected by your lesson. He (she) wants to know if when he (she) dies, will he (she) go to hell?" What was gleaned out of the other 1,000 sermons on grace, the church, heaven, the plan of salvation. Christ, God, etc.? We don't know. Young people don't talk as much about those lessons. For some reason, sermons on hell get their attention while sermons on forgiveness do not. There is the side of God that is characterized by grace, mercy, forgiveness, protection, and deliverance that needs to stick in the minds of young people as well as the wrath of God for sin.

There is definitely a place for Ruth Ann Howell's book, Blessed Assurance. I can imagine its being used to great benefit in Bible classes in Churches of Christ. I wish that denominational people would open their minds and read it too. The message is clear, biblical, and needful. Members of the Lord's church surely need to live in the confidence and boldness that Jesus died to give us. Sister Howell has done a good job of bringing us that truth from God's word and illustrating it in such a way that makes it greatly appreciated. Read her notes carefully. Practice the exercises at the end of each chapter. Study the appendices and make proper application. You will be the better and happier for it.

Andy Kizer

Ruth Ann Howell is a member of the Summerdale Church of Christ in Summerdale, Alabama. Recently, she asked me if I would write a forward for her book. It is my pleasure to do so.

No one is more interested in the saving of souls than Ruth Ann. She has conducted classes for the women of the Summerdale Church on personal evangelism. Souls have been saved as a result. One time she met a man in a doctor's office. She set up a study and the man obeyed the gospel.

While she is concerned for the salvation of the others, she has had a struggle with her own "Assurance of Salvation". This has been a journey of many years. Finally, she is at peace. Now she wants to share that peace with others.

She realizes that once a person is saved, he can so live as to be lost (Acts 8:18-24). However, she has learned that it is equally true that we can "STAND IN GOD'S GRACE" (1 Peter 5:12). We stand in his grace by "Walking in the Light" (1John 1:7). The one who walks in the light will no longer have his sins chalked up against him. (Romans 4:8). Furthermore, the one who walks in the light is no longer condemned (Romans 8:1). What "blessed assurance" this is.

Ruth Ann has laid out the road that leads to that assurance. Please read of her long struggle toward a peace that passes all understanding (Philippians 4:7).

If you were asked, "Are you saved?" How would you answer this question? We can "KNOW" (1 John 2:3). This book will help you to understand how you can know for sure about your salvation.

Billy Lambert
Minister
Summerdale Church of Christ
Summerdale, Alabama

Table of Contents

Chapter 1: "An Un-fulfilled Need" 1
Chapter 2: Initial Salvation 7
Chapter 3: "Laundry Day Syndrome" 13
Chapter 4: The Search For Security 17
Chapter 5: Grasping and Getting a Grip on Grace 23
Chapter 6: Does God Really Care? 27
Chapter 7: Jesus Loves Ruth Ann Howell: THIS I know! 33
Chapter 8: But He Giveth More Grace 37
Chapter 9: More Precious Than Gold 41
Chapter 10: A Matter of Being Faithful 47
Chapter 11: Getting the Monkey Off Your Back 53
Chapter 12: If Ye Continue 59
Chapter 13: When Time Shall Be No More 63
Appendix 1: Pertinent Scriptures 71
Appendix 2: Suggestions For Further Reading 75
Appendix 3: How God Saves and Keeps Us 77
Appendix 4: Outline For Open Bible Study 81
Appendix 5: What Must I Do To Be Saved? 83
Appendix 6: God's Master Plan for Salvation 87
Appendix 7: Poems by Kevin Patrick Dillon 91
Acknowledgements: 95
Biography: 96

Chapter One
"An Un-fulfilled Need"

"That being justified by His grace, we should be made heirs according to the hope of eternal life" (Titus 3:7).

Ruth Ann sat in her Bible class as a teenager in the 1950's. Negative...negative...negative! "Thou shalt not..." "Hell is horrible, and you don't want to go there." "Straight is the gate and narrow is the way and few there be that find it." These are all truths, but it was missing the glorious truth of the joy of one's salvation and the wonderful blessings we have in Christ.

These were the lessons I did not receive:
• How can I grow and mature as a Christian?
• Heaven is indeed real and reachable.
• God's commandments are not grievous (1 John 5:3).
• Teach me to pray.
• God expects only our reasonable service (Romans 12:1).
• Help me see how God answers prayers.
• Since I cannot be perfect, how can I be saved?
• God's grace is sufficient for me (2 Corinthians 12:9).

Being Christians, you have probably sung Blessed Assurance, I Know My Name Is There, and I know Whom I Have Believed, as well as many other hymns that proclaim the assurance of salvation. Yet deep in our hearts, we doubt our own salvation.

There was a time in my life when if someone asked me if I was saved I probably would have said, "Well, I hope so." Yet, if one had asked a denominational person the same question, she would have said, "Yes, I certainly am." Why would that person want to trade her certainty and joy for my uncertainty and misery? At that time in my life, to reply that I was certain I was saved would have made me feel that I was bragging, puffed up, and conceited. Now I know that to reply "yes" to that question indicates that my God keeps His promises. He never lies; it is impossible for God to lie (Hebrews 6:18). According to 1 John 2:3-4, we can know we are saved. *"Now by this we know that we know Him, if we keep His commandments. He who says, I know Him, and does not keep His commandments, is a liar, and the truth is not in him."*

I went through trials, doubts, and turmoil in a quest to understand how I could be absolutely assured of my salvation. I learned that this assurance does not spring from conceit, egotism, or self-righteousness, but from trust in the promises of God, who never lies and always keeps His promises. I hope that by the end of these lessons you will know as I know that by remaining faithful in the love of God through submission and obedience to Him that God will welcome us to our home in heaven where we will abide forever with Him and all the saints (Revelation 2:10).

I had never been taught to feel compassion for my fellow human beings who were lost, without hope, and without Christ. Yet I felt miserable and unsure of my salvation while my denominational friends were full of certainty. It didn't make much sense to try to convert them from the security they felt to join me in my misery.

I reasoned, *"Faith without works is dead"* (James 2:26b). So I set out to chalk up some good works and earn my way to heaven; otherwise, I would surely be lost. God's grace was foreign to my thinking. My youth was stuffed full of preaching, Bible classes, and religious activities, but my spiritual needs were not being met.

I had never been shown the positive attributes of God, though I knew the negative side all too well. While the Bible contains many "Thou-shalt-nots," one needs a healthy balance of both positives and negatives, much like the opposite sides of a magnet.

By the 21st century, the pendulum had swung away from the negative. Most sermons were positive sermons about heaven and eternal life for the true child of God. The old "hell-fire" sermons are rare in the present day preaching. We still need to know about the negative, but it must be tempered with the beauty and the wonder of heaven, eternal life, and our hope in Christ. One without the other makes the Christian's life unbalanced and confused.

The fear of God and the knowledge that He will indeed punish the disobedient motivates us to become His children. If we fear and revere God, we can learn to love Him for *"perfect love casteth out fear"* (1 John 4:17-18). Our relationship with our heavenly Father is much like the one with our earthly father. When out of love our fathers discipline and punish our disobedience, we learn to revere, fear, and love him. So it is with our Father in heaven.

How desperately we need to know God's abiding love, grace, and mercy toward us! We must learn that we can have assurance that we are saved. Denominations teach their members that they must accept Christ in their hearts as their "personal savior" and that the saved cannot be lost. But the Bible clearly refutes this belief: *"Brethren, if anyone among you wanders from the truth, and someone turns him back, let him know that he who turns a sinner from the error of his way will save a soul from death and cover a multitude of sins"* (James 5:19-20). As I matured, I learned that to give a definite affirmative answer to the question -- Are you saved?" -- is not bragging on yourself. Rather, the affirmative answer shows confidence in the promises of God and shows faith that we trust Him to keep those promises. God does not want us to be in constant turmoil. He doesn't want us to be afraid, upset, or unsure of our salvation.

"By that will we have been sanctified through the offering of the body of Jesus Christ once for all" (Hebrews 10:10).

When by baptism for the remission of your sins (Acts 2:38), you become a Christian, all your sins are forgiven (remitted) through contacting the blood of Christ during baptism. You become a child of God through the new birth of water and the Spirit, and God adds you to His family, the church (Acts 2:47). You know you have become a Christian because you have been obedient to the Bible's teaching on salvation. When you do as the Bible teaches concerning salvation, you can be assured of your salvation. How can we know that we know God? 1 John 2:3 tells us: *". . . and hereby we do know that we know Him if we keep His commandments."* God wants you to be assured of your salvation, and by trusting in God's word and in His promises, you can know you are saved. And after becoming a Christian, you can stay saved through further obedience to His word.

MEMORY VERSE: *"If we walk in the light, as He is in the light, we have fellowship one with another, and the blood of Jesus Christ, His son cleanseth us from all sin"* (1 John 1:7).

My prayer is that you will realize the great blessings you have in Christ and that you will want to share this knowledge with your friends.

NOW...LET'S OPEN THE BIBLE.
(The KJV was used in this exercise.)

1. God shows two things unto the heirs of promise, and He confirmed it by an oath (Hebrews 6: 17-19).

    A. It was _____ for God to _____.

    B. We have strong consolation (encouragement) who have fled for refuge to _____ _____ upon the _____ set before us; which _____ we have as an _____ of the soul, both _____ and _____, and which _____ into that within the _____."

2. (2 Peter 3:9) " The _____ is not slack concerning His _____. God is _____ to us-ward, not _____ that any should _____, but that all _____ come to _____."

3. (2 Timothy 3:16-17) "All Scripture is given by _____ of _____ and is profitable for _____, for _____, for _____, for _____ in righteousness: That the _____ of God may be _____ (complete); thoroughly furnished unto all _____ works."

4. (Romans 6:17-18). "But _____ be thanked, that ye were the _____ of _____, but ye have _____ from the heart that _____ of _____ which was

_____ you. Being made _____ from _____, ye became the _____ of _____."

5. (Romans 4:20-23). "Abraham _____ not at the _____ of God through _____, but was strong in _____, giving _____ to _____; and being fully _____, that, what God had _____, He was able also to _____. And therefore it was _____ to him for _____."

NOTE: We are saved by God's grace through faith. We are not saved by our own good works, our good moral life, by being a good neighbor or citizen, by paying our debts, and certainly not because we deserve to be saved. If such things could save us, Christ's death on the cross would have been unnecessary and in vain.

6. (Ephesians 2:8-10) "For by _____ are ye _____ through faith; and that not of _____: it is the _____ of _____: Not of _____, lest any man should _____. For we are His _____, created in Christ Jesus unto _____ _____, which God hath before _____ that we should walk in them."

7. (James 2:17) "Even so faith, if it _____ _____ works, is _____, being alone."

8. (James 2:18) "Yea, a man may say, Thou hast faith, and I have _____ ; shew me thy _____ without thy _____

and I will _____ thee my faith by my _____."

9. (James 1:22) "But be ye _____ of the _____, and not _____ only, deceiving your own _____."

10. (James 2:26) "For as the _____ without the spirit is _____, so _____ without _____ is _____ also."

FOR DISCUSSION

1. Why do you think in the 1940's so much of the preaching was negative?

2. How does negative preaching affect our view of God?

3. Why is it important for little children to understand the "loving Father concept" of God?

4. Why do we need to hear positive and negative preaching in a balanced program?

5. Are heaven and hell equally effective motivations for obedience to God?

Chapter Two
Initial Salvation

"Whoever denies the Son does not have the Father either; he who acknowledges the Son has the Father also. Therefore let that abide in you, which you heard from the beginning. If what you heard from the beginning abides in you, you also will abide in the Son and in the Father. And this is the promise that He has promised us—eternal life" (1 John 2 23-25) NKJV.

Initially you were saved because you followed the steps that lead to salvation. You heard the gospel, which produced faith. Romans 10:17 says, *"Faith comes by hearing, and hearing by the word of God."* You believed in God's word, and you believed that Jesus is the Son of God, born of Mary, a virgin who miraculously conceived by the Holy Spirit. You were convicted of your sins as the guilt of your trespasses weighed heavily on your soul. This led you to repent of your sins, just as many of the Jews repented when Peter and the apostles preached to them concerning their guilt in the death of Jesus in the first gospel sermon. In baptism, you emulated Christ's death, burial, and resurrection. It was in baptism that you contacted the blood of Christ that washed away your sins. Your old self died to sin. You came from the waters with a clean slate ... white as snow ... no ugly marks, raised to walk in newness of life. In your baptism, you received the gift of the Holy Spirit (Acts 2:38).

At the point of baptism, you were simultaneously born into God's family, SAVED, added to God's church (Acts 2:47). Your name was written in the Book of Life (Revelation 20:12), and you became an heir of God and joint-heir with Christ (Romans 8:17). All spiritual blessings became yours (Ephesians 1:3). You received Christ's promise, *"I will never leave you nor forsake you"* (Hebrews 13:5b). You obtained the assurance of a heavenly home.

MEMORY VERSE: *"Likewise reckon ye also yourselves to be dead indeed unto sin, but alive unto God through Jesus Christ our Lord"* (Romans 6:11).

HEAR THE GOSPEL

Matthew 28: 19-20 "Go ye therefore, and _____ _____ _____, _____ them in the name of the _____, and of the _____, and of the _____ _____: _____ them to observe _____ _____ whatsoever I have _____ _____: and, lo, I am with you _____, even unto the _____ of the _____. Amen."

Romans 10:13-14 "For whosoever shall _____ upon the _____ of the _____ shall be saved. How then shall they _____ on him in whom they have not _____? and how shall they _____ in him whom they have not _____? and how shall they hear without a _____?"

BELIEVE THE GOSPEL

In John 8:24, Jesus said, "I said therefore unto you, that ye shall _____ in your _____: for if ye _____ _____ that ___ am _____, ye shall _____ in your _____."

Hebrews 11:6 "But _____ _____ it is impossible to _____ ____: for he that cometh to God must _____ that ____ ____, and that ____ is a rewarder of them that _____ _____ _____."

Luke 6:46 "And why call ye me, _____, _____, and do not the _____ which I _____?"

Hebrews 5: 8-9 "Though he were a _____, yet _____ he _____ by the things which he _____; And being made _____, he became the _____ of _____ _____ unto _____ them that _____ Him;"

REPENT OF YOUR SINS

Luke 13:3 "I tell you, Nay: but, _____ ye _____, ye shall all _____ _____."

Acts 17:30 "And the _____ of this _____ God _____ ___; but now _____ all men every where to _____:"

Acts 2:38 "Then Peter said unto them, _____, and be _____ every one of you in the _____ of _____ _____ for the _____ of _____, and ye shall receive the _____ of the _____ _____."

CONFESS YOUR FAITH

Matthew 10:32 *"Whosoever therefore shall confess me before men, him will I confess also before my Father which is in heaven."*

Acts 8:36-37 *"And as they went on their way, they came unto a certain water: and the eunuch said, See, here is water; what doth hinder me to be baptized? And Philip said, If thou believest with all thine heart, thou mayest. And he answered and said, I believe that Jesus Christ is the Son of God."*

BAPTIZED INTO CHRIST

Mark 16:15-16 *"And he said unto them, Go ye into all the world, and preach the gospel to every creature. He that believeth and is baptized shall be saved; but he that believeth not shall be damned."*

1 Peter 3:21 *"The like figure whereunto even baptism doth also now save us (not the putting away of the filth of the flesh, but the answer of a good conscience toward God,) by the resurrection of Jesus Christ:"*

Acts 22:16 *"And now why tarriest thou? arise, and be baptized, and wash away thy sins, calling on the name of the Lord."*

Galatians 3:27 *"For as many of you as have been baptized into Christ have put on Christ."*

Romans 6:3-4 *"Know ye not, that so many of us as were baptized into Jesus Christ were baptized into his death? Therefore we are buried with him by baptism into death: that like as Christ was raised up from the dead by the glory of the Father, even so we also should walk in newness of life."*

Colossians 2:12 *"Buried with him in baptism, wherein also ye are risen with him through the faith of the operation of God, who hath raised him from the dead."*

NOW LET'S OPEN THE BIBLE
Find the verse, and answer the question according to the scripture.

1. HEBREWS 11:6

What is necessary to please God? _____

2. ROMANS 10:17

What comes by hearing the Word?_____

3. ROMANS 10:9-10

What part of man believes unto Righteousness? _____

4. LUKE 13:3&5

What is the 8th word in each of these two Verses? _____

5. JOHN 18:31-37

Whose confession of Christ was more a question than a statement?

_____

6. GALATIANS 3:27

Into whom are we baptized?_____

7. 1 PETER 3:21

According to this verse, what saves us? _____

8. ACTS 2:47

To what does the Lord add the saved?_____

SCRIPTURES TO STUDY

• "Jesus said to him, "I am the way, the truth, and the life. No one comes to the Father except through Me" (John 14:6).

• "Or do you not know that as many of us as were baptized into Christ Jesus were baptized into His death? Therefore we were buried with Him through baptism into death, that just as Christ was raised from the dead by the glory of the Father, even so we also should walk in newness of life" (Rom. 6:3-4).

• "... being justified freely by His grace through the redemption that is in Christ Jesus" (Romans 3:24b).

Chapter Three
"*Laundry Day Syndrome*"

"For I will be merciful to their unrighteousness, and their sins and their iniquities will I remember no more" (Hebrews 8:12).

You just washed that pretty white kitchen apron yesterday, but one misfired squirt from that yellow plastic mustard bottle and it's back to the laundry room again. The blood of Christ is not like laundry detergent. Detergent may be applied today, but tomorrow it has to be applied all over again when little Mattie Grace wipes her peanut butter and jelly-covered hands on it.

Christ's blood is unlike any other cleansing agent. Christ's blood has the power of continual cleansing. I am not teaching the doctrine of "Once Saved, Always Saved." According to Galatians 5:4, it is possible for us to fall from grace: "You have become estranged from Christ, you who attempt to be justified by law; you have fallen from grace." So every time I fail in word or deed, am I lost? Do I fall in and out of the grace of God every time I falter?

A key verse escaped me in my early years as a Christian. How I wish I had understood 1 John 1:7: "But if we walk in the light as He is in the light, we have fellowship with one another, and the blood of Jesus Christ His Son cleanses us from all sin."

Pretend you are driving down the Interstate, and suddenly a big black bird splatters your windshield with blueberries. Do you panic? No. You just turn on the window washers and wipers. As you drive further down the road, bugs hit your window. What did one bug say to the other as he hit the windshield? Bet you don't have the guts to do that again. Again the wipers come to the rescue. Next time it is fog, then rain, sleet, and mud thrown up by a semi-truck that rushed by you. Those wipers wipe and wipe, and you can still see your way clear. My point? As long as we continue in Christ, living faithfully with Him in the church, He will constantly and repeatedly cleanse us from our sins with His blood. HOW I LOVE MY CLEAR, CLEAN WINDSHIELD!!!

Write the memory verse from lesson one in the space below. _____

_____

_____

_____

_____

Your trust and confidence in God and your knowledge of His mercy and grace assures you that God cannot lie and that He always keeps His promises.

Your task now is to hold on to your reward of eternal life. You can do this by loving God and keeping His commandments, being loyal to His word, and living a pure life. You must love both the brethren and your enemies. If you remain faithful in God's service to the end, you are promised a "Crown of Life" (Revelation 2:10). You must know that heaven is real and attainable for all true believers. The burdens we must bear for the Lord are not grievous (1 John 5:3), and the admonition to present our bodies as living sacrifices is our reasonable service (Romans 12:1). We must keep in mind everything that He has done for us.

Stay true to God's Word, the Bible, and follow the teaching delivered by the apostles. The Bible tells us that if anyone brings a new gospel and seeks to divide the body, we are to mark that one and avoid him (Romans 16:17).

Temptations will happen. You are not alone in your temptation. Even the Lord underwent temptation. But God tells us that He will not allow us to be tempted beyond that which we can bear (1 Corinthians 10:13). Just know that with every temptation, the Lord provides a way of escape (1 Corinthians 10:13). My friend, Margaret Epperson, a faithful Christian remarked once, "Our problem is that we do not look for the way of escape." We need to be watchful because Satan is like a duck on a June bug, ready to devour Christians, especially babes in Christ.

Should we willfully go back into the sins of the world? The Bible tells us that for us to return to worldly ways is like a dog returning to his own vomit. When we return to sin after becoming a Christian, we are like a hosed-off pig, wearing her county fair blue ribbon, that returns home and plops in the mud-hole (2 Peter 2:22). Yet, as Christians, when we do stumble into sin, we have an advocate with the Heavenly Father, and there is a second avenue of pardon available to us, that of repentance and of prayer. We are welcome to return to God and to the full fellowship of His saints, and to the church. We can repent, have our sins forgiven, and continue our faithfulness to God unto death (Revelation 2:10b).

While our life in Christ is a fight against evil, it is also a life of joy and of love and is rewarding in countless ways. From the prison dungeon in Rome, the beloved apostle Paul wrote to Timothy, his son in the faith, that the time of his departure from this earth was near. He wrote, " I have fought a good fight, I have finished my course, I have kept the faith: *"Henceforth there is laid up for me a crown of righteousness, which the Lord, the righteous judge, shall give me at that day: and not to me only, but unto all them also that love his appearing"* (2 Timothy 4:7-8). When we live as we should, we just can't wait for Jesus to take us home.

MEMORY VERSE: *"And we know that all things work together for good to them that love God, to them who are the called according to His purpose"* (Romans 8:28).

CHRISTIAN ADVENTURE PROJECT

This week, be aware of situations during which you experience temptation. Look for the mode of escape the Lord provides. There will always be an escape route! But you have to be ready and look for it! (1 Corinthians 10:13)

SCRIPTURES TO STUDY

• (Romans 5:8) But God commendeth his love toward us, in that, while we were yet sinners, Christ died for us.

• (1 John 4:10) Herein is love, not that we loved God, but that he loved us, and sent his Son to be the propitiation for our sins.

• (Hebrews 8:12) For I will be merciful to their unrighteousness, and their sins and their iniquities will I remember no more.

DISCUSSION

1. What is Laundry Day Syndrome?

2. Explain how the blood of Christ is like a windshield wiper.

3. Read the six short chapters of Galatians. What caused the Galatians to fall from grace?

4. Research the apostle Paul. What are some of the trials he endured in his life?

5. Why do you think the apostle Peter used such graphic illustrations of the dog and the pig to describe a Christian who returns to the lusts of the flesh?

Chapter Four
The Search For Security

In my search to find the answer to my heart's desire to be absolutely certain of my salvation, I diligently read the scriptures, soaking them into my life. It wasn't enough just to know what the Bible said, I had to make it part of Ruth Ann Howell. This was an individual study for me because to that point I had not found what I was seeking in sermons and classes.

WRITE THE MEMORY VERSE FROM LESSON TWO HERE: _____
_____
_____
_____

Have you ever heard of a Piranha? It is a small freshwater fish that inhabits South American rivers, and what a voracious appetite it has! Perhaps it will help you to imagine that you are an Ocean-going Olympic medalist piranha and the Bible is a tasty whale!

Just for fun in this chapter, I will be Ruth Ann Piranha.

Ah...Here is Ruth Ann piranha, famous Olympic gold medalist, protein-eating piranha. I am swimming laps up and down the South American coastline. My eyes are trained to look for potential delectable treats. My fins and tail race through the waters at record-breaking speed because of my strict exercise regimen. The blue Atlantic water is especially clear today, and I am ravenously searching for a tasty dinner. I will not be satisfied with skimpy crabs or shrimp. No, today I must have a full-course, hearty meal, complete with dessert!

Suddenly from the surface above me, the waters grow eerily dark. It is a great whale. A deafening splash from its monstrous tail creates waves of havoc for miles in every direction. I am stunned and taken aback. My gills flutter quickly and my tiny heart pounds. "Yes!" I shout in my brave and eager fish voice. "Dinner at last!" There is no fear in my soul. I know what I want, and I'm going after it! Zoom, zoom! Contact with the target. Thrashing about. Behold, the skeleton of a great whale. Victorious piranha! (Please excuse the burp.) Story ends.

NOW... LET'S OPEN THE BIBLE

Find Psalms 37:4, our memory verse: *"Delight thyself also in the Lord, and He shall give thee the desires of thine heart."* Let's think about the piranha for a moment. I think the absence of a certain trait in Ruth Ann Piranha is the difference my sister Sue noticed in me. What was that missing quality? FEAR! The piranha was tiny, and the whale huge, but fear was not a factor, and Ruth Ann Piranha got what she wanted. Do you remember me telling you that in the past I had lived in fear that I would mess up and that God would snatch me up and cast me into hell? What took away my fear? The answer almost sounds too simple.

MEMORY VERSE: *"Delight thyself also in the Lord. He shall give thee the desires of thine heart"* (Psalms 37:4).

SCRIPTURE ALERT!

The following scripture must be read and digested before proceeding further: *"There is no fear in love; but perfect love casteth out fear, because fear hath torment. He that feareth is not made perfect in love. We love Him because He hath first loved us"* (1 John 4:18-19).

I want you to know that God is not a big scary troll who wants to punish you! God is a loving Father who created you in love and wants only what is best for you! When we can understand and believe that, we will be able to relax and enjoy the relationship we have with our heavenly Father. God does not want to cast anyone into torment. God doesn't want anyone to be lost; however, each person is a "free moral agent." The irony of it is that when John in Revelation 21:8 lists the types of people destined to be cast into hell, the first ones he mentions are the fearful. That kind of fear has got to go! If you will love God, that fear will be cast out.

With my fear gone, my assurance of salvation became part of my life, my existence, and my very being. I became content and satisfied. My life felt like the peaceful song of a bird after an immense storm had passed. I felt as if I had been wrapped in God's caring arms and that He loves me as a unique and special person who belongs to Him! Reality dawned! I am God's child, and He is my heavenly Father. If I were the only living creature on this earth, He would still have sent His Son Jesus to die for me so I could escape the sin and sorrow of this earth.

The big picture is that I plan to live for God now, and one day I will see His face and live with Him forever. This is not a dream nor a wish but a lifestyle of reality. Life with God will help you face each day with a renewed zeal. Heaven IS attainable, but you must make the choice to love God, to cast out fear, and to stay on course.

JUST FOR FUN

1. Make a list of the five people you love the most.
2. Mark an X by any person you once feared.
3. Mark an O by any person you no longer fear.
4. Now ... let's talk about what made the difference.

Friends may turn on us. Our families may experience injury or devastating disease. And each one of us will sooner or later see the casket of a loved one lowered into the earth. Like gold that is liquefied, rid of all its impurities, and then solidified into precious and beautiful metal, we are tempered by the trials we endure on life's road. We are strengthened by life's twists and pitfalls, and by our trials we are given strength, endurance, and courage to overcome all that we must in this life.

"Ye are in heaviness through manifold temptations: That the trial of your faith, being much more precious than gold that perisheth, though we be tried with fire, might be found unto praise and honour and glory at the appearing of Jesus Christ" (1 Peter 1:6b-7).

In spite of what may befall us, Jesus has promised to be with us always (Matthew 28:20). His love for us motivates Him to be faithful to us, and our love for Him demands that we hold His hand through every circumstance. We know where we are going, and we know how to get there. Let's feel secure in the knowledge that He is with us every step of the way, even through the valley of the shadow of death. *"Yea though I walk through the valley of the shadow of death, I will fear no evil: for Thou art with me"* (Psalms 23:4a).

In 2004, I visited a sweet lady in the Intensive Care Unit just hours before she died. She was a Christian lady, but she looked scared. I took her hand and looked into her frightened eyes, and I told her, "Everything is going to be okay." She replied, "Do you think so?" "Yes," I said, "Everything will be okay."

When we replace fear with love, security allows us to face the trials of each new day. This security brings zeal, bravery, and indescribable confidence. Peace and contentment rush to fill the void that is there when we let go of fear. With fear banished, God assures us that no matter what heartache, trouble, test, sickness, or grief invades our sphere of activity, all will be well. We should thank the Lord for this security, because we will certainly need security as we live in this troubled world.

Each of us will be tried and tested. Strange crises and unusual events will come our way. Longtime friends may disappoint us.

I'm not sure if the lady in the intensive care unit totally understood my message, but I was speaking of the other side ... Heaven ... her eternal home where the faithful will gather for eternity. I'm reminded of the story of the angels carrying Lazarus the beggar into Abraham's bosom (Luke 16:22). I believe she needed assurance as she crossed to the other side. The death of a Christian will be swallowed up in Victory. As the apostle Paul asked in 1 Corinthians 15:55, *"O death, where is thy sting? O grave, where is thy victory?"*

The security a Christian enjoys lasts through every trial and experience of life, including our final hours as we approach death. Now, I realize that a Christian's assurance of salvation is necessary for contentment and happiness, but it is also necessary to face life's tribulations and hardships. Assurance of salvation is a lifestyle like no other! After you have worked out your own salvation with fear and trembling and have discovered the answers you sought, you will find that you possess something extra special in the blessings found only in Christ Jesus (Ephesians 1:3).

You have but to click on the TV to see the pitiable state of the world's affairs. Just look through your church membership directory and see how many faces have left the church. Many are good moral decent people, but many good moral decent people are lost. Your own blessed assurance motivates you and compels you to explain to the lost the blessings in Christ

Jesus. And you will want others to have the security you have because that will instill in them a desire to restore those who have fallen away. I think that many who leave the church never fully understand the joy and blessed assurance of salvation.

Something is wrong with me if my joy and gladness does not spill over into sharing Christ with others. Though I walk on this earth and live here, I do not belong here. My citizenship is in heaven. I am not alone! God, Christ, and the Holy Spirit are in me, and glad songs in my heart cheer me on my way upward. This certainty of salvation is priceless. Many seek happiness, but cannot find it because they are seeking it in the wrong places. How can I share this joy with those who do not have a clue what they are missing? Oh, if I could just make them realize the marvelous satisfaction there is to be found in Christ.

I am growing old and have wrinkles and gray hair. I am much closer to "the other side of Jordan" than I was in my youth, yet I look forward to seeing God's face, to beholding Christ's appearance in the clouds, and being a part of the great reunion in the sky with Noah, Moses, Peter, Lydia, my aunt and many others. *"Though the outward man perish, yet the inward man is renewed day by day"* (2 Corinthians 4:16b). This scripture is framed and hangs on the wall of Dr. Stephen Collier's office waiting room in Florence, Alabama.

DARE TO COMPARE: Compare Ecclesiastes 12:13 to John 14:15 & John 15:14. Does the light go on in your head?

Match the text to the Scripture reference:

A. Colossians 3:15 _____1. *"And let the peace of God rule in your hearts, to the which also ye are called in one body; and be ye thankful."*

B. Philippians 4:7 _____2. *"And the peace of God, which passeth all understanding, shall keep your hearts and minds through Christ Jesus."*

C. Philippians 4:6 _____3. *"Be ye careful for nothing, but in everything by prayer and supplication with thanksgiving, let your requests be made known unto God."*

MEMORY VERSE: *"But as it is written, Eye hath not seen, nor ear heard, neither have entered into the heart of man the things which God hath prepared for them that love Him"* (1 Corinthians 2:9).

CHRISTIAN ADVENTURE PROJECT

Read the entire book of Jonah. Don't panic; it is a short book. As you read through Jonah's story, try to identify what his motivation was. Was it fear? Was it selfishness? What caused Jonah to change his mind? Do you think his motive ever changed? Do you think Jonah could have benefited from this book?

Be prepared to discuss this in next week's class.

SCRIPTURES TO STUDY

• *"Every good and perfect gift is from above, and cometh down from the Father of lights, in whom there is no variableness, neither the shadow of His turning"* (James 1:17).

• *"God is not a man that He should lie ... Hath He spoken and shall He not make it good?"* (Numbers 23:19a and c).

• *"The Lord is not slack concerning His promise, as some men count slackness, but is long suffering to us-ward, not willing that any should perish, but that all should come to repentance"* (2 Peter 3:9).

Chapter Five
Grasping and Getting a Grip on Grace

MEMORY VERSE: *"For by grace are ye saved through faith; and that not of yourselves. It is the gift of God, not of works, lest any man should boast"* (Ephesians 2:8-9).

Aruba is a desert island situated off the coast of Venezuela. Though only 21 miles long, Aruba is rich in lizards, cactus, rocks, and sand. The weather is generally hot because Aruba is very near the equator. You can get sunburned in only a few minutes. Rain is a rare thing on the island.

The Roman Catholic Church has built a little church on the top of a hill in Aruba. Leading up to the top of the hill are "Twelve Stations of the Cross" to which sinners may crawl on their knees one level at a time to do penance for their sins. At the pinnacle of the climb, a sign with an arrow points to "Refreshments and Barbecue." We might find this to be laughable at first, but it isn't funny, and it is so typical of man's thinking through the ages. Idol worshippers sacrificed to appease their false gods. The doctrine of selling indulgences (paying in advance for the privilege of committing sin) greatly increased the wealth of the Catholic Church. I heard a story about a schoolteacher in the 1960's who told her students that when they appeared before God in the Judgment that the good scale had better outweigh the bad. God knew long ago that people would reason like this. The phrase "not of works" in Ephesians 2:9 should be enough to set us straight. Salvation cannot be earned. It is obtained by grace through faith. It is God's gift.

When I was a little girl, an extra excitement flooded my emotions when I received a gift from a certain friend. She was a person whose demeanor I admired, and she had a history of always giving very special gifts. I could hardly wait to open one of her gifts. God is the giver of every good and perfect gift (James 1:17). We know God's goodness through His gifts to us.

What is the gift of grace that God gives? The first people to hear a gospel sermon were devout Jews from every nation who were gathered in Jerusalem on the first day of the week for Pentecost, about 2000 years ago. When they asked what they ought to do to rid themselves of the guilt they felt for putting God's Son to death on the cross, the apostle Peter told them, *"Repent and be baptized, every one of you, in the name of Jesus Christ, for the remission of sins, and ye shall receive the gift of the Holy Spirit"* (Acts 2:38). And many of them were baptized (Acts 2:41), which saved them (1 Peter 3:21), and the Lord added them to the church (Acts 2:47). God granted them salvation from their sins, a perfect gift from a perfect giver! The Jews could not earn their salvation. Neither they nor any man could ever repay God for putting His perfect Son to death on the cross. What man could not do, God did for him by giving him the wonderful gift of salvation.

Neither you nor I can earn our salvation; however, there is something we must do to obtain it. We must accept His gift by rendering obedience to God's instructions. The postman can leave a package for you in the mailbox, but unless you get it out of the mailbox and open it, you cannot have access to its contents. We accept God's gift by repenting of our sins and being baptized for remission of those sins. (See Luke 13:3-5; and Acts 22:16)

"Who hath saved us, and called us with an holy calling, not according to our works, but according to His own purpose, and grace, which was given us in Christ before the world began" (2 Timothy 1:9).

"That in the ages to come He might show the exceeding riches of His grace in His kindness toward us through Christ Jesus. For by grace are ye saved through faith: and that not of yourselves; it is the gift of God" (Ephesians 2:7-8).

CHRISTIAN ADVENTURE PROJECT

Give a neighbor an unexpected gift this week, maybe flowers from your yard, cookies you have baked, or something you have made. Note her response. Does she seem grateful? Do you think she feels indebted or obligated to you? Compare your neighbor's response to the gift you gave her to how you feel about God's gift to you!

QUESTIONS THAT WILL NOT WASTE YOUR TIME

1. According to Ephesians 1:3, where are all spiritual blessings?

2. Read Hebrews 4:16. How may a Christian approach God's throne?

3. Find all the words in Hebrews 10:19-23 that begin with the letter "b" and draw a circle around the one that was used as a purchasing agent.

4. In 2 Timothy 4:6-8, Paul looked forward to receiving something that you and I might also receive. What was it?

5. Look up the word "persuade" in the dictionary. Using that definition, what would you say about Paul's confidence toward Christ in 2 Timothy 2:21?

6. *"But the God of all grace, who hath called us unto His eternal glory by Christ Jesus, after that ye have suffered a while, make you perfect, stablish, strengthen, and settle you"* (1 Peter 5:10). How are we called by the grace of God?

RESEARCHING GRACE IN THE SCRIPTURE

Read the Scripture selections on grace below. Determine whether they are true or false, and mark T or F in the space provided.

Remember, regardless of our opinion, the Bible is always right!

1. _____ Titus 2:11 ... At one time God's grace had appeared to all men.

2. _____ 1 Peter 5:10 ...Those who receive God's Grace will never again suffer.

3. _____ Ephesians 2:8 ... We are saved by faith only.

4. _____ 2 Thessalonians 2:16 ... Consolation and hope come through grace.

5. _____ Romans 3:23 ... Not everyone has sinned.

6. _____ Hebrews 4:6 ... We should be very frightened to approach God's throne.

7. _____ Ephesians 1:7 ... Redemption and Christ's blood is associated

with God's grace and Christ's blood."

8. _____ Titus 3:7 ... Being Justified by grace is necessary to having the hope of eternal life.

9. _____ Acts 20:32 ... Grace can build you up.

10. _____ 2 Timothy 1:9 ... Grace was God's plan before the world was made.

FOR DISCUSSION

Read Acts 20:32. What are the two things grace will do for us?

Read Romans 11:5-6. If works cannot save a man, why do Christians even bother to do good works (Also see Ephesians 2:10)?

Chapter Six
Does God Really Care?

My parents were killed in a twin-engine Cessna plane crash in June of 1963. They were in their early 40's and in the prime of their lives, at the very peak. I was 22 years old and had been married to David, my husband for four years. We were married on May 29, 1959. My first born, Ginger, was three years old and my baby Dianna was only one when their grandparents were suddenly whisked away by death. This tragedy was very hard on my family.

David had been working with Daddy for the L.C. Fuller, Jr. Lumber Company in Haleyville, Alabama. There were so many problems working with governmental agencies. For David, dealing with those agencies was a nightmare, and we finally closed down the company. We almost lost everything we had, but we never gave up on God or turned our backs on the church.

From my dad, I inherited persistence, tenacity, and boundless energy. Daddy would pick the brains of very smart people. He asked many questions of them. He was a seeker and a visionary. I inherited these traits from him.

Mama was the role model from whom I learned to build strong faith. Because of her example, I developed a love for the Lord and for His church. I also inherited her courage. When it came to standing against evil and standing for the right, she stood as straight as an arrow and as tall as a pine tree. Mama wasn't a "huggy-kissy" type. I remember her going about her housework and daily chores with great diligence. Mama had a presence, and everyone felt it when she was around. Mama's feelings for her faith and her family ran deep, and though verbalization was difficult for her, she would have fought a herd of elephants for us girls.

But my parents were gone, and having married at the tender age of 18, I was still wet behind the ears and had much to learn. David and I learned from each other, and we kept our faith in God. We moved ever forward to make a life for ourselves.

When my sister Sue was only 30, she was diagnosed with a brain tumor.

This, of course, had a great impact on my life, as did many other things that space will not allow me to mention here. The facts that I have mentioned will suffice to let you know that I have experienced heartaches, trials, and tribulations in my life. I learned to lean on God and to trust Him. I know what it is like to experience difficult circumstances, but I know that God will not burden us with a heavier load than we can bear. 1 Corinthians 10:13 states, *"There hath no temptation taken you but such is common to man; but God is faithful, who will not suffer you to be tempted above that ye are able; but will with the temptation also make a way to escape, that ye may be able to bear it."* Let me assure you that if you have had problems in your life, I can empathize with you. I know how illness, death, and loss of possessions can wear you down and make you sad. Let me lead you to the knowledge that God does really care. Trials and tribulations will come your way. No one is immune! *"Man that is born of woman is of few days and full of trouble"* (Job 14:1). If you haven't experienced troubles yet, they may be just around the corner.

I remember Mama singing church songs when she went about her chores, and I hated it! I hated to hear her sing! Now I do the same thing! Isn't that crazy? Maybe ... maybe not. The great apostle Paul said, *"I have learned, in whatsoever state I am, therewith to be content"* (Philippians 4:11). That was probably the reason Mama sang. James gives us another reason to sing: *"My brethren, count it all joy when ye fall into diverse temptations; knowing this, that the trying of your faith worketh patience. But let patience have her perfect work, that you may be perfect and entire, wanting nothing"* (James 1:2-4).

I do not think it is an accident that my faith in God is much stronger now and that I am happier and feel secure in my salvation. The rocks along the path of my life were but stepping stones to contentment! Because of trials, tests, and tribulations that David and I have endured and continue to endure, we are stronger in spirit. Life's problems aren't what sinks your boat...it is the way you deal with them! You have the choice! You can trust God and lean on His promises with the knowledge that "...this too shall pass," or you can blame God for all your problems. Will you become "bitter or better?" This is an important choice because many have given up on Christ and His church. This might not have happened if they had developed the proper attitude.

At times, I fall into one of those moods, and words just flow out of my heart through my pen onto paper. At other times, I don't know what to write or what to say, but I believe it is God's will and His desire that this book be made available for those who need it. When I taught this material in a Ladies' Class, the ladies encouraged me, telling me that the lessons helped them and that they had used the lessons to help others. I pray that these lessons glorify God and help you to do the same!

Sometimes following Jesus involves reaching out for His hand and holding on for dear life. What were the promises He made? *"Lo, I am with you always, even to the end of the world"* (Matthew 28:20), and *"I will never leave you nor forsake you"* (Hebrews 13:5). Mama never taught me that I couldn't fly, and nothing but death could stop my dad from reaching his goals. I was taught to believe that I could do anything. If I set my mind on it and tried with all my might, I could accomplish it. Just keep on trying. Don't take 'no' for an answer. Never give up has always been my philosophy, and "I can't" has never been part of my vocabulary.

This brief chapter of my personal struggles was written to help explain what makes me tick. I feel that knowing some of my history and background will help you to understand where I am coming from. I feel driven to get this message out, to lift some and to encourage others, to lend a hand to a wayward Christian, to give hope to the discouraged, and to help a Christian find contentment and happiness. My fervent prayer is that this message will help an alien sinner to find the way to salvation.

MEMORY VERSE: *"Casting all your care upon Him; for He careth for you"* (1 Peter 5:7).

MULTIPLE CHOICE QUESTIONS
(Select the correct answer)

1. The trying of our faith causes us to have:
a) depression b) despair c) dread d) patience

2. Read Philippians 1:19. Paul knew that his imprisonment would turn out for:
a) his salvation b) his detriment c) his death d) punishment for his sins

3. According to 2 Corinthians 3:17, Where the Spirit of the Lord is, there is:

a) license b) limitation c) listlessness d) liberty

4. Read 1 Thessalonians 4:17-18. Knowing that Christ will return to take us to heaven should cause the Christian to have:
a) comfort b) fear c) laxity d) zeal

5. In 1 Thessalonians 3:7, Paul said that while he was in affliction and distress, he was comforted by other Christian's:
a) generosity b) gifts c) patience d) faith

6. Read Luke 21:1-3. Who gave the most to God?
a) Gentiles b) rich men c) armies d) poor widow

7. Mark 4:19 says the cares of this world:
a) choke the word b) refute the word c) deny the word d) divide the word

8. In 1 Corinthians 9:9-10, what animal is used to prove that God really cares about people?
a) sheep b) doves c) oxen d) fish

9. In Luke 10:34, what two medicines did the Good Samaritan use to heal the wounds of the stranger for whom he cared
a) oil and vinegar b) wine and salve c) oil and wine d) Hyssop and myrrh

10. David's dilemma in Psalms 142:4 was that no man cared for his:
a) Army b) children c) wife d) soul

CHRISTIAN ADVENTURE PROJECT

Ask God to help you become aware of another person's need, and then do what you can to show that person you really care. For example, you might drive an elderly person to the doctor, help a student with homework, or just be a good listener to a troubled soul as they pour their heart out to you.

SCRIPTURES TO CONSIDER

"For ye have not received the spirit of bondage again to fear; but ye have received the Spirit of adoption, whereby we cry, Abba, Father. The Spirit itself beareth witness with our spirit, that we are the children of God: And if children, then heirs; heirs of God, and joint-heirs with Christ; if so be

that we suffer with him, that we may be also glorified together" (Romans 8:15-17).

"For I am persuaded, that neither death, nor life, nor angels, nor principalities, nor powers, nor things present, nor things to come, nor height, nor depth, nor any other creature, shall be able to separate us from the love of God, which is in Christ Jesus our Lord" (Romans 8:38).

Chapter Seven
"Jesus Loves Ruth Ann Howell" THIS I Know!

Were I the only sinner left on earth, God would send Jesus down to die for me. Jesus would come of his own free will. This is true because I am one of the "whosoevers" in John 3:16-17.

Those who hang crucifixes on walls have done a great disservice to mankind. God is not pleased with graven images used in worship (Remember the Ten Commandments). The thought of hanging Jesus on a wall. Seriously? Who of you would make a statue of a loved one who had died a horrible death and hang their image on a wall? When we hang things up, they become common and forgotten. When the crucifix is used as an icon for the masses to teach that Jesus is the Savior of mankind, the intimate and personal side of an individual's relationship with Christ is down-played. Hanging Jesus on a wall does not seem personal.

When one hails Jesus as the Savior of the masses, He seems so far away. True, He is the Savior of all those who believe in Him and obey His commandments. And though it sounds denominational to say, "Jesus is my personal Savior" (so many false doctrines have been attached to this statement), He is just this. However, until He becomes intimately personal to you, He will be afar off. If the great joy of knowing you are saved is what you seek, take Christ into your heart. Let Him live there, be your best friend and guide you in all your endeavors. You will no longer be your own; you will be His! *"What? Know ye not that your body is the temple of the Holy Ghost which is in you, which you have of God, and ye are not your own? For ye are bought with a price; therefore glorify God in your body, and in your spirit, which are God's"* (1 Corinthians 6:19-20).

God loves everyone, and that is a fact. Nevertheless, He loves you and me personally if we have put on Jesus. He knows our middle names and the sum of the hairs on our heads! My God is my friend. He is my Savior. He is my king, my shepherd, my joy, and my everything. The Almighty God gives detailed attention to me every day of my life. He becomes more real to me every, day and talking to Him daily is sweet conversation. My worship to Him is not a dull, lifeless, ritualistic practice of going through meaningless motions, but an innate adoration of my own God who knows me intimately. All He requires of me now is to, *"do justly, to love mercy, and to walk humbly with Him"* (Micah 6:8).

The O'Neal Bridge in North Alabama spans the Tennessee River and joins Colbert and Lauderdale Counties. Suppose you were driving in a car across that bridge one day and you saw a man dumping millions of dollars from a briefcase over the bridge and into the murky waters below. Either you stop him or someone will. "What are you doing?" you shout. "Getting rid of my wife's soup labels." he says. "Those aren't soup labels! Those papers are U.S. currency, worth millions of dollars!" While this is an unthinkable example, the lesson here is that people often do not realize the value of what they have.

Our soul's salvation is worth infinitely more than ten million dollars, and yet people throw it away because they do not realize the precious value of their soul! Your soul is priceless. If we, with joy, daily converse with Jesus our friend, we can look forward to going to heaven to live with Him. There will be no more pain and suffering, no more tears and all will be beautiful and enjoyable for eternity!

Why do you suppose people throw away their salvation? I think they just do not understand what they have. People leave the church of our Lord because they feel that God is impersonal and that He is too remote to care for them. When a person feels like that, they begin to reason, "Well, if God doesn't care about me, why should I live for Him? I'll just move on."

Sadly, in my earlier life, I had that mindset. God was distant to me. I obeyed the gospel to avoid being "fried" in hell, not because I loved Him. Having an impersonal God was just not satisfying. This relationship was damaging me, but my sister, Sue, noticed it, and I am sure others noticed also. Though I attended worship and church activities, I had what might be termed "low levels of rejoicing" and this is probably an understatement of the actual truth. I went about with a sad face and a troubled heart. Sue could see that there was no joy in my religion. Why was I chronically uncomfortable? Soon, Sue became grateful when I didn't bring up the subjects of God, religion, or the Bible. She did not want to share in my misery. Again I say, "Why would anyone secure in their denominational religion want to leave their security and come to be miserable with me?

And then like a magnificent strobe light, I discovered the meaning of God's grace! Salvation was a gift from God because He loved me, not something I had to earn by doing good deeds, and if I didn't do good deeds I would be bound for torment. God desires for me to enjoy my life every day with all the spiritual blessings in Christ Jesus (Ephesians 1:3). Like a sponge, I began to absorb the knowledge of the kind, loving Father I had. He wanted me to succeed and was rooting me on. God truly cares about Ruth Ann Howell, and Jesus, the carpenter went to heaven to build me a very special place to spend eternity. I discovered the value of what I possessed! I knew I had it! I wanted to cling to the bubbling joy that the promises God had made me. Sharing the gospel became my desire, not a chore!

At that point, Sue noticed a change in my outlook, and she was "pleasantly pleased." If Sue could see the difference in me, surely people in the world could take note of how Christ changes the lives of Christians.

That is the reason for this book: Getting Christians to know, to really know that gift they have and to possess that gift with excitement and admiration for the indescribable value and joy of salvation that it brings. Christianity is a way of life. It is living in a positive direction, with a pathway illuminated by the light of God's glorious Word.

Jesus loves me, this I know
Took too long to learn it though.
Now my life is filled with song,
'Cause to Jesus I belong.

FOR DISCUSSION

1. Discuss Mark 4:38. Did the storm help Peter to have more faith in Christ? With Jesus asleep on a pillow, was Peter right to think that Jesus did not care? What did Jesus do to change the situation?

2. Read Matthew 5:43-48. Tell what God does that proves He loves everyone.

3. Does Romans 8:28 say that all things are good? If we want things to work out right, what should we do, according to this verse?

4. Discuss Romans 8:1, and write it on this blank. _____
_____
_____

5. Read Matthew 6:25ff. Using the examples Jesus gave of the birds and the lilies, explain how we know God cares for us (Matthew 6:26-28).

6. Behold what manner of love the father hath bestowed on us, that we should be called the sons of God." (1 John 3:1a)

MEMORY VERSE: *"But He giveth more grace. Wherefore He saith, God resists the proud, but giveth grace unto the humble"* (James 4:6).

Chapter Eight
But He Giveth More Grace

I know we have had one chapter on grace, but notice "more grace" in the memory verse. There is much more to grace than I could ever comprehend. How could the God who dreamed, schemed, and invented all the workings of the universe have even a brief interest in a country Alabama girl named Ruth Ann? But He Does!!!!

Grace is not something you pull off a tree and eat. It is not an artifact you dig up, put on a pedestal, and behold. *"Therefore, being justified by faith, we have peace with God through our Lord Jesus Christ: by whom also we have access by faith into this grace wherein we stand, and rejoice in the hope of the glory of God"* Romans 5:1-2.

Did you get that? If you are like me, you definitely didn't get it all in your first reading of the New Testament. That is because you must become as humble as a lowly, hole-filled sponge. You must imbibe the biblical idea of grace by reading passage after passage, meditating on the thoughts and clues provided you by the inspiration of the Holy Spirit through the word of God. And even if you don't become thoroughly saturated, you will still be able to make a nice splatter. (I hope you get this abstract picture I am painting. Imagine that you are the sponge and the subject of grace, and grace is the water you are soaking in.) Oh well, let it soak in a while.

You don't have to get the grace concept all at once, for the Bible says, *"But grow in the grace and knowledge of our Lord and Savior Jesus Christ. . ."* (2 Peter 3:18a). It takes sunrises and sunsets to grow children, but once they have attained maturity, we look back with wonderment as to where all the time went. But we do need to get growing! Life is short, and eternity is ... well, it is forever!

The Galatian Christians quickly fell away from the grace of Christ into a perverted gospel. (Galatians 1:6-9) The apostle Paul instructed and urged these Christians to put off the works of the flesh and to develop the fruits of the Spirit (love, joy, peace, longsuffering, gentleness, goodness, faith, meekness, and temperance) Galations 5:22-23. Bearing this fruit is an outward manifestation of a soul that is growing in grace inwardly. Though not a perfect definition, grace is defined by some as unmerited favor. We do not deserve salvation. For our sins, we deserve death! "But thanks be to God for His unspeakable gift! Christians need never worry that they have enough grace. He always has enough! God says, *"My grace is sufficient unto thee"* (2 Corinthians 12:9). Friends, I have got it made if I am in the grace of God. That certainly does not mean that I will not have trials or suffering. I certainly will. Even if I should have to face torture or death for my faith in Christ, I will not feel threatened with death! Eternal heavenly bliss awaits the faithful Christian for all they have undergone.

So cling to the precious treasure of salvation by grace through faith in Christ. Remember, salvation is not of works, lest anyone should boast of the number of hospital visits they have made, how many sermons they have preached, how many miles they have traveled on mission campaigns, or how many alien sinners they have taught and baptized. We were created to do good works, but we do not earn our salvation with them (See Ephesians 2:8-10).

Grace allows me the liberty and freedom to relax and feel at home with God. Being God's child by adoption (Romans 8:15 & Galatians 4:6), I can address Him as "Abba" (An affectionate term of endearment) and boldly come to God's throne of grace. I can ask Him for grace to help in time of need and not have to fear that He is going to criticize me for asking. In fact, Jesus encouraged asking. In the famous Sermon on the Mount, He said, *"Ask, and it shall be given unto you"* (Matthew 7:7).

Please understand what I am saying on this subject. Everybody does not enjoy the benefits of grace. In Acts, chapter two, the Jews in Jerusalem on the day of Pentecost received the gift of the Holy Spirit when they believed, repented, confessed, and were baptized for the remission of their sins. Then the Lord added them to His church (Acts 2:47). Those who refuse to repent and obey will not enjoy God's gift of grace. Being saved by grace does not mean that we abandon all discipline and do everything we want to do.

What shall we say then? Shall we continue in sin, that grace may abound? God forbid. How shall we, that are dead to sin, live any longer therein? Know ye not, that so many of us as were baptized into Jesus Christ were baptized into his death? Therefore we are buried with him by baptism into death: that like as Christ was raised up from the dead by the glory of the Father, even so we also should walk in newness of life (Romans 6:1-4).

Note three more important things that Romans 6 teaches:

1. We are not under law but under grace (Romans 6:15)
2. We should thank God that by our obedience we ceased to be servants of sin and became servants of righteousness. (Romans 6:16-22)
3. The gift of God is eternal life through Jesus Christ our Lord (Romans 6:23).

An erroneous notion is that if we preach grace too much, church members will become lazy. But the truth is that a saved-by-grace child of God will enjoy and use his freedom to pray, think, love, give, serve, and worship. The real danger is being sucked into a philosophy which teaches that the more Bible chapters we read each week, the more visitors we bring to church, the more youth rallies we attend, guarantees us more brownie points on our scorecard, and then God will just let us into heaven if we get on our knees and beg, "Please, please, let me enter into the pearly gates!" A thousand times, "NO"! Salvation is by grace through faith--not by works. Salvation is the gift of God, bestowed on those who have obeyed from the heart that form of doctrine delivered to them. Paul certainly did not become lazy because he was saved by grace (Romans 6:17).

"But by the grace of God I am what I am: and his grace which was bestowed upon me was not in vain; but I laboured more abundantly than they all: yet not I, but the grace of God which was with me" (1 Corinthians 15:10).

QUESTIONS THAT WILL NOT WASTE YOUR TIME

1) By whom do we have access into grace (Romans 5:1-2)? _Christ_

2) In what other than grace must we grow (2 Peter 3:18)? _knowledge_

3) To whom does God give grace (James 4:6)? _humble_

4) What is the quality of God's grace (2 Corinthians 12:9)? _sufficient unto thee_

5) For what reason were we created (Ephesians 2:8-10)? _____
To do good works that God prepared for us to walk in the
we (do not earn) our salvation
6) What is the gift of God (Romans 6:23 and Acts 2:38)?
eternal life in Christ Jesus our Lord. Repent & be baptized
for the remission of sins; & you shall receive the gift of the Holy Spirit

7) What is the seven letter word in 1 Corinthians 15:10 that is a synonym for Worked? Labored (more abundantly than they all, yet not I, but the grace of God which was with me)

8) According to Ephesians 1:2, where is grace?
Grace to you and peace from God our Father, and the Lord Jesus Christ

9) Read Hebrews 13:9. With what thing should the heart be established?
Do not be carried about w/ various & strange doctrines for it is good
that the heart be established by grace, not with foods which have not
profited those who have been occupied with them.

10) Name two great things that accompany grace, according to 1 Timothy 1:14? and the grace of our Lord was exceedingly abundant, with faith
& love which are in Christ Jesus.

MEMORY VERSE: *"But the God of all grace, who hath called us unto His eternal glory by Christ Jesus, after that ye have suffered a while, make you perfect, stablish, strengthen, settle you"* (1 Peter 5:10).

PROJECT OF THE WEEK

Using a good dictionary, obtain as many definitions for grace as you can. You will likely find at least eight. List them here:

1. _____
2. _____
3. _____
4. _____
5. _____
6. _____
7. _____
8. _____

Chapter Nine
More Precious Than Gold

In the negative era of "fear God and fear hell," life was unbalanced for me. The positive was scarcely heard. Like positive and negative sides of a magnet, people need both positive and negative preaching to maintain a balanced and healthy spiritual diet. Likewise, our bodies need a little fat to burn to provide vital energy in lean times, but too much fat can cause obesity, lipid problems, and heart disease. Romans 11:22 instructs us to *"behold the goodness and severity of God."* To have a true picture of God, we must look at both sides of the coin.

The negative preaching I heard while I was growing up was detrimental because it destroyed the atmosphere of Christian joy, making it impossible for love and kindness to thrive. During the later era of almost all-positive preaching, we got so comfortable that we turned inward, became lazy, and church growth declined. We stopped being concerned about the lost souls around us. Personal evangelism efforts dwindled.

I knew that *"faith without works is dead, being alone"* (James 2:17), and I knew that the denominational concept of "once saved ... always saved" was wrong as well, according to Galatians 2:16. It just seemed logical that I should go about doing good works. In my mind, these good works were deemed to be on the good and positive side of God. Subconsciously, I believed that my constant benevolent activities were paving my way to Heaven. I expected of myself a certain number of good works each week, and if I fell short of my expectations, I felt guilty. This became a vicious circle. The guiltier I felt, the more good works I thought I needed to do to make up for the shortfalls. Hence, my activities began to snowball. I surmised that I needed to visit the sick, to call those who missed worship, to take meals to the bereaved and to those coming home from the hospital. I felt I must pray at least three or four times daily. I constantly browbeat myself for falling short and not doing more. It became overwhelming! I later realized that this is the same concept held by the Jehovah's Witness group, who are sent out from their Kingdom hall with assignments to do as they work their way to heaven.

In retrospect, I realize that I expected more of myself than God did, and thus I could not enjoy my Christian life. My motivation for staying on the straight and narrow road originated from fear of punishment in hell for displeasing God. In my mind, I thought I was doing the right thing. I tried to attend all church services, even when I was sick. With all this activity stemming from fear rather than love, I was making myself sick. The fact was, my desire to avoid hell was much stronger than my craving to go to heaven.

Romans 12:1-3 talks about grace, thinking soberly, and our reasonable service to God. When we understand God's grace, we are able to think soberly, and we realize that God does not expect more of us than we can do. The parable Jesus taught about the men with varying amounts of talents supports this. He required each servant to be responsible for only what was entrusted to him. All too often, we are harder on ourselves than God is! In Matthew 11:28-30, Jesus comforts us with these words, *"My yoke is easy and my burden is light."* God wants us to be happy and to enjoy His blessings here on earth as we walk in the footsteps of Christ. He does not expect us to trudge around in misery for the duration of our stay in this world and defer all joy until the hereafter. *"Now the God of hope fill you with all joy and peace in believing, that ye may abound in hope, through the power of the Holy Ghost"* (Romans 15:13).

So many people look for happiness, contentment, and peace in all the wrong places. They seek fame, fortune, popularity, pleasures, and the vices of this world. Consider the number of people who have all these things and still commit suicide. In Ecclesiastes 12:13, Solomon tells us the secret of a fulfilling life, and he also reveals the purpose for our existence here on this earth. I hear people say, "I need to go find myself," when I didn't even know they were lost!

MEMORY VERSE: *"Let us hear the conclusion of the whole matter: Fear God, and keep His commandments: for this is the whole duty of man"* (Ecclesiastes 12:13).

I guess the way you sum up the works vs. grace issue is this: "You can't go to heaven without good works, but you can't work your way to heaven or earn your passage there." It almost seems like a paradox, doesn't it?

The apostle Paul's longing to go and be with Christ near the end of his life is beautiful.

For I am now ready to be offered, the time of my departure is now at hand. I have fought a good fight, I have finished my course, I have kept the faith: Henceforth there is laid up for me a crown of righteousness, which the Lord, the righteous judge, shall give me in that day; and not to me only, but unto all them that love His appearing. (2 Timothy 4:6-8)

Here Paul refers to himself as the "chief of sinners." This same man who suffered as many persecutions as any man in history refers to the crown he hopes to receive as a gift from the Lord, not something that he had earned. Think about that.

Remember, to be balanced, we need both the positive and the negative. Though the Christian life is one of joy and blessings that promises the ultimate reward, we must endure trials and temptations on our trip to glory.

Wherein ye greatly rejoice, though if need be now for a season, though ye be tried with fire if need be, ye are in heaviness through manifold temptations: That the trial of your faith, being much more precious than gold that perisheth, though it be tried with fire, might be found unto praise and honour and glory at the appearing of Jesus Christ. (1 Peter 1:6-7)

SIN TAKES YOU FARTHER THAN YOU WANT TO GO, KEEPS YOU LONGER THAN YOU WANT TO STAY, AND COSTS YOU MORE THAN YOU WANT TO PAY!

You can only advance in the direction you are facing. Therefore, look toward heaven. In John 14:6, Jesus said, "I am the way, the truth, the life; no man cometh unto the Father but by me." In 1 John 1:7, John wrote, "But if we walk in the light as He is in the light, we have fellowship one with another, and the blood of Jesus Christ cleanseth us from all sin." The word "cleanseth" denotes a continual cleaning. The blood of Jesus continually cleanses us from all sin.

At this point, it is important for us to understand the nature of sin. Sin is the transgression of God's law, and it separates us from God. In our initial obedience to God, when we believed in Jesus Christ, repented of our sins, confessed Christ before men, and were baptized, all our sins were washed away. (See Acts 22:16; Galatians 3:27; 1 Peter 3:21 and Romans the 6th chapter) Those sins are gone, as far from us as east is to west, as if God buried them under the floor of the deepest ocean.

But what about the sins we commit after baptism? Please note that there are two types of sins. One is the sin that we inadvertently commit, meaning that we did not sit up all night planning the sin. For example, I might be at home alone running the vacuum in my kitchen, stub my toe on the table leg, and let an ugly word slip out. Does that mean I must be baptized all over again? No! God knows I am not perfect. In my humility, I realize that I have sinned, so I repent and pray, "Dear Heavenly Father, I am very sorry I did that. Help me not to do it again." And He forgives me.

Or I might have an evil thought. I can't keep birds from flying over my head, but I can keep them from building nests in my hair. That is what walking in the light has to do with. When we are converted to Christ and are really trying to do His will every day, we generally have our lives steered in the right direction. Of course, we are not perfect, and we will most certainly mess up once in a while. That is what grace is for! Christ's perfect sinless life makes up for all our inadequacies. After all, He died to forgive us, and as long as we comply with the conditions of forgiveness, He will keep forgiving us. *"And their sins and their iniquities will I remember no more."* (Hebrews 10:17)

A second kind of sin is the deliberate sin. Suppose I decide on Monday that I want to go down to the local bar and pick up a man next Saturday night. So I go over all the details in my mind of how I will do it. I go to town and buy a provocative looking outfit, some enticing cologne, and splurge on all new cosmetics. On Friday, I get a new perm. On Saturday, I get all dolled up and make my grand entrance. I sit at the bar and drink until I am absolutely plastered. I know all along that this is wrong, but I want to do this. I am selfish. Of course, I do not read my Bible all week because I do not want to encourage any guilt feelings.

Let's make a point of just how gross and disgusting sin really is. Peter gave two graphic illustrations of how disgusting it is when a Christian leaves the path of righteousness and returns to the sin of the world. First, a Christian who returns to sin is like a dog that returns to his own vomit and eats it. Second, a Christian who returns to sin is like a pig that has been washed and runs back to wallow in the filthy mud hole. Not pretty pictures! (2 Peter 2:22)

[handwritten: CHRIST STEPS "Who committed no sin nor was deceit found in his mouth."]

Can a member of the church who has sinned in a public way have forgiveness for their sin? For our answer, let's turn to the scripture. In Acts 8, Simon the sorcerer sinned in a public way when he tried to buy the power of the Holy Spirit. He was rebuked for this, and was told that he should repent and pray for forgiveness. (Acts 8:22) James instructs Christians to "confess your faults one to another, and pray for one another, that ye may be healed. The effectual fervent prayer of a righteous man availeth much." James 5:16

Then there is the story of the Prodigal Son that Jesus told in Luke 15: 11-24. The son left home, wasted his inheritance, came to himself, repented, and returned home. Was the father glad to see him when he returned home? Yes! He ran to meet him. He gave him new shoes, a ring, and a robe. He killed the fatted calf and held a party for his son who was alive and had returned. The beauty in the story of the Prodigal Son is that the son represents us and the father represents our God, our Heavenly Father who runs to meet us with open arms.

SCRIPTURES TO STAND ON

"If we walk in the light, as He is in the light, we have fellowship with one another, and the blood of Jesus Christ His Son cleanseth us from all sin" (1 John 1:7).

"God commendeth His love toward us, in that while we were yet sinners, Christ died for us" (Romans 5:8).

"Being justified freely by His grace through the redemption that is in Christ Jesus, Whom God hath set forth to be a propitiation through faith in His blood, to declare His righteousness for the remission of sins that are past, through the forbearance of God" (Romans 3:24-25).

"And now, little children, abide in Him; that when He shall appear, we may have confidence and not be ashamed before Him at His coming" (1 John 2:28).

FOR DISCUSSION

- Read Acts 8 and tell how many people were involved in the sin that Simon committed.

- Did Simon's sin involve more than just an evil thought?

- Find the Prodigal Son's statement of confession in Luke 15:17-18. Who did the boy admit sinning against? *"I have sinned against heaven & before you."*

- Is the righteous man in James 5:16 a sinless person? Give other scriptures that back up your answer.

- Why is there a need to confess public sin? *James 5:16 Confess your sins one another*

- Psalm 51 recounts David's prayer for forgiveness and confession of sin. Read this aloud in class to get a feel for the depth of his remorse and penitence. Why do you think David was called "a man after God's own heart"?

MIRROR, MIRROR ON THE WALL

1. Read James 1:22-25. What might a Christian see if he looks into the perfect law of liberty, the mirror of God's Word?

2. Why is it so difficult for us to admit that we have sinned?

3. After reading Romans 3:23, do you think the knowledge that all have sinned makes it easier for a person to repent.

4. How are we justified according to Romans 3:24?

5. What two things are contrasted in Romans 6:23?

6. According to 2 Timothy 3:16-17, where would a person look to find out how to correct a mistake that he had made? *The scriptures — Doctrine, Reproof, correction & instruction — equipped for every good work*

7. Using 2 Timothy 4:2, can you prove, that both positive and negative preaching is needed?

8. Read Psalm 139:1-14. If God knows all our thoughts, why do we still need to confess our sins to Him?

9. Herein is our love made perfect, that we may have boldness in the day of judgment, because as He is, so are we in this world." (1 John 4:17) How can we have boldness on the day of judgment? *in this; that we may have boldness in day of judgment because as He is so are we in the world. Love has been perfected among us in this;*

Chapter Ten
A Matter of Being Faithful

The simple casket contained the body of an old man whose name will not be remembered by many. Few attended his funeral service. The elderly fellow left behind no fame, no unique inventions, and no wealth. He never wrote a book or recorded a hit song. No spectacular trophies adorned the shelves of the home he left behind. The preacher pointed out to those who attended the old man's funeral that God does not require fame, popularity, and wealth, but that our God requires faithfulness (1 Corinthians 4:2).

The deceased man was a Christian husband. It does not matter that society will not erect a monument to him or even remember his name. God knows his name and will reward his faithfulness. The writer of Proverbs 22:1 says, *"A good name is rather to be chosen than great riches, and loving favour rather than silver and gold."*

James F. Wyres, at this writing, is the minister of the Winfield Church of Christ in Winfield Alabama. Many years ago, he found an outline by Guy N. Woods and used it at the Freed-Hardeman College Lectureship in Henderson Tennessee. From that outline and the influence of Gus Nichols of the Sixth Avenue Church of Christ in Jasper Alabama, Wyres began to realize for the first time that our salvation is "not a matter of perfection, but of being faithful." I am much indebted to him for the ideas in this chapter.

What we could not do for ourselves, Christ has done for us. He became sin for us and died in our place, thus freeing us from condemnation. *"There is therefore now no condemnation to them which are in Christ Jesus, who walk not after the flesh, but after the spirit"* (Romans 8:1).

Those who follow Christ faithfully can be secure in their salvation. The emphasis on faithfulness excludes those who are lackadaisical as well as those who are openly rebellious against God. It is important to note the two scriptures below that prove this point: *"What shall we say then? Shall we continue in sin, that grace may abound? God forbid. How shall we, that are dead to sin, live any longer therein?"* (Romans 6:1-2).

"Therefore we ought to give the more earnest heed to the things which we have heard, lest at any time we should let them slip. For if the word spoken by angels was steadfast, and every transgression and disobedience received a just recompense of reward; how shall we escape, if we neglect so great salvation; which at the first began to be spoken by the Lord, and was confirmed unto us by them that heard him…." (Hebrews 2:1-3).

Houseplants die when we do not water them faithfully. We faithfully feed ourselves to maintain nutrition, to alleviate hunger, and to provide the energy we need to be active. Unfaithfulness can end marriages. Unfaithful employees can destroy a business. Do you get the point?

Let's focus on the faithfulness of God for a moment. Every day, His sun rises to bless the earth. Every year, the seasons return in their courses. In each moment, we have air to breathe. Yes! God is faithful! He is always there! If God can be trusted to provide us with such material necessities, can we not also believe the promises He makes in His word regarding the salvation of our souls?

CONSIDER SOME OF GOD'S PROMISES

1. He will not forget our work and labor of love (Hebrews 6:10).

2. He has given unto us all things that pertain to life and godliness (2 Peter 1:3).

3. God is true (2 Corinthians 1:18).

4. God will hear your prayers in your closet and reward you openly (Matthew 6:6).

5. God's peace will keep your hearts and minds through Christ Jesus (Philippians 4:7).

Earlier in the book, I discussed the preachers of the "negative era" who probably preached what they believed to be the needs of the people of that day. As a result, many Christians grew up and lived without the assurance of salvation. Without the emphasis on the continual cleansing of the blood of Christ (1 John 1:7), they may have been discouraged enough to throw away their Bibles and cry. It is easy to understand how many became frustrated with knowing they could never be perfect, and that a lifetime of good deeds could not earn them salvation, especially if God's grace was omitted from the preaching they heard.

The Jews had this problem! They believed that observance of the Law of Moses would save them, but at the same time they were aware that they could not keep the law. They, too, were miserable. (Read the 7th chapter of Romans.) Even though they may have desired to keep the law, their ability to do so was lacking because of the weakness of the flesh. The carnal mind cannot please God (Romans 8:5-8). Yet, if the Spirit is in us, we are not in the flesh but in the spirit. Note Paul's Question of despair with regard to this subject, and his immediate sigh of relief with its answer. *"O wretched man that I am! Who can rescue me from the body of this death. I thank God through Jesus Christ our Lord. So then with the mind I myself serve the law of God, but with the flesh, the law of sin"* (Romans 7:24-25).

It is the faithfulness of God that saves us when with our willing minds, we, though imperfect people, serve Him faithfully. Faithfulness is much easier to identify than to measure. Like baking a cake, if you put in all the right ingredients and follow the directions, you will obtain the desired results. The duration of our faithfulness to God is "unto death." *"Fear none of those things which thou shalt suffer: behold, the devil shall cast some of you into prison, that ye may be tried; and ye shall have tribulation ten days: be thou faithful unto death, and I will give thee a crown of life"* (Revelation 2:10). The reward is "a crown of life." No man, having put his hand to the plough, and looking back, is fit for the kingdom of God (Luke 9:62).

EXERCISE IN FAITHFULNESS

1. What are two things God is faithful to do for you? (2 Thessalonians 3:3)
    a. _Establish you_
    b. _Guard you from the evil one_

2. What can we surmise about the Colossian Christians from reading? Colossians 1:2? _To the saints + faithful brethren in Christ who are in Colosse. Grace be to you + peace from God our Father + the Lord Jesus Christ._ FAITHFUL

3. In light of what we have studied thus far, why is it important to trust God's faithfulness? (See 1 John 1:9) _____
_____
_____
_____

IDENTIFY THE FAITHFUL BY NAME

Faithful Minister: (Colossians 4:7) _Tychicus, beloved brother_

Faithful Brother: (Colossians 4:9) _Onesimus & beloved_

Faithful High Priest: (Hebrews 2:17) _Jesus_

Faithful Witness: (Jeremiah 42:5) _____

Faithful Martyr: (Revelation 2:13) _____

Faithful Man: (Nehemiah 7:2) _____

FOR DISCUSSION

Give reasons why faithfulness is necessary in each of the following relationships:

1. Husband to Wife _____
_____

2. Doctor to Patient _____
_____

3. Teacher to Pupil _____
_____

4. Parent to Child _____
_____

5. Employee to Boss _____

_____

6. God to You _____

_____

7. You to God _____

_____

Chapter Eleven
Getting the Monkey Off Your Back

My dad once gave me a pet monkey. I loved Nippy! He was so much fun. Nippy had quite a personality. He would join me in my playhouse, and I would give him ice cream. He would pick at my sister's legs, and he would slap her if she tried to stop him. Sometimes Nippy would get loose, and we would have to recruit the whole neighborhood to catch him.

Dad had an office in our basement. That crazy Nippy managed to crawl through ductwork and gain entrance into the office while we were gone. He got into Dad's ink and made the biggest mess of that office you can imagine. When we got home and saw that mess, I thought, "O Boy, I have had it now!" After all, Nippy was my responsibility. Although I enjoyed Nippy as a pet, his behavior became generally too bothersome, and finally we loaded him up and gave him to the Birmingham Zoo. As it turned out, the other monkeys did not like him.

There is a spiritual lesson of the utmost importance to be learned from my experience with this monkey. Though the monkey gave me pleasure at first, his shenanigans began to trouble my family and our neighbors. When Nippy created chaos of my dad's orderly office, strained relations developed between Nippy and me. What I am trying to say is this: Sometimes we are much better off if we completely rid ourselves of the "monkey."

Let us lay aside every weight that doth so easily beset us, and let us run with patience, the race that is set before us (Hebrews 12:1b). Sin is a weight, like a monkey on our back. Sin is a distraction. We are supposed to keep our eyes on Jesus (Hebrews 12:2), which is more difficult if you have to chase monkeys and clean up after one. Notice that the Scripture says to lay aside every weight. Our pet monkeys (pet sins), however many there are, need to be cast aside. This will free us to focus on Christ and to make following Him our goal.

At the point of baptism, Jesus saved us from all our past sins by washing them away (1 Peter 3:21; Acts 22:16). We have discussed the Christian's responsibility to walk in the light, and we understand that as long as we do this, Christ's blood continually cleanses us. We are told to remain faithful unto death (Revelation 2:10b). Nevertheless, it is possible for a Christian to lose or throw away his salvation (2 Timothy 4:10). Demas loved the world more than he loved God, and he forsook his service to Christ. The church in the region of Galatia fell from grace (Galatians 5:4). Since we are not perfect, God made a plan to remedy the sins that could potentially entrap us after baptism. There are two types of sins that warrant discussion here.

Private Sins: From time to time, a Christian might have an evil thought, might view things that should not be viewed, or might smoke a cigar behind the barn, any of these without participation or knowledge of anyone but the Lord. Though no one else on earth may know what we have done, God is all-knowing and is aware of every secret thought and every secret deed. For these sins, a Christian must be truly repentant and ask for God's forgiveness in prayer. The book of Isaiah says, *"Thou wilt keep him in perfect peace, whose mind is stayed on Thee"* (Isaiah 26:3).

Public Sin: Public sins are those sins known by others. These sins cause shame and bring reproach on the church. James instructs Christians to confess their faults one to another and to pray for one another to be healed (James 5:16). A solid example of this "second law of pardon" is found in Acts 8:9-24. After his baptism, Simon the Sorcerer expressed an evil desire to purchase the power of the Holy Spirit with money. He was told to repent and pray. Simon did ask for prayer.

Sins may be further categorized as "accidental" or "pre-meditated." It is important that we know how to deal with these sins. Accidental sins are not planned or pre-meditated. For example, one might lose his temper and utter an expletive. Grace and mercy come into play here, as the Christian makes confession with such sins. By private prayer, we can return to walking in the light. The blood of Christ washes away this sin as a windshield continually cleans the car window.

On the other hand, willful (pre-meditated) sins are those planned in advance in full knowledge that they are sinful. Suppose a church member decides to forsake the assembly of the church in order to participate in a bass fishing tournament. Gassing up his boat, paying for a fishing license, buying bait, and filling his thermos with coffee are evidences that this Christian has planned to forsake worship. Hebrews 10:25-27 is a clear indication that this is willful, planned in advance, pre-meditated sin and must be dealt with according to how well known the sin is. This must be repented of either publicly or privately.

Sin is heavy. Sin is deceptive. The sin may appear light, frivolous, and fun. When lust conceives, it brings forth sin. When sin is finished, it brings forth death (James 1:15). The sin of adultery in the passion of the moment seems pleasurable. In the weeks to come, the evidence of a venereal disease may erupt, or pregnancy may result. Then there may be a child involved. There may be a break-up of two homes. The list goes on and on.

Though King Solomon had more wisdom than any man before him or since, he rebelled against God by allowing his wives to lead him into idolatry. His willful sin became public. There might have been a tragic end to his life. "For the wages of sin is death; but the gift of God is eternal life through Jesus Christ our Lord" (Romans 6:23).

Many track stars and distance runners use ankle weights while they train, but they never use them on the day of the big event. They remove the ankle weights and their legs feel lighter, thus helping them psychologically and physically. Before I understood the concept of "no condemnation" to those who are in Christ, to those who walk in His light and grace, the biggest monkeys on my back were worry, doubt, and anxiety. What heavy weights they were! Once I threw them off, I began to really enjoy my Christian life. *"There is no condemnation to them which are in Christ Jesus"* (Romans 8:1). This applies to the baptized believer that remains faithful to the end of their life.

From our study of the scriptures, we have learned that our salvation is NOT A MATTER OF PERFECTION but one of BEING FAITHFUL UNTO DEATH (Revelation 2:10). God will give the faithful a "Crown of Life." This is an awesome blessing and one of "great relief."
In the Sermon on the Mount, Jesus taught us that if we seek His righteousness first, we will be provided with whatever food and clothing we need (Matthew 6:33). In the same sermon, He admonished us not to be anxious about tomorrow. Many of the weights we carry around with us are so unnecessary, and Jesus didn't put them on us. We put them on ourselves. Worry is a lot like a rocking chair. It gives you something to do, but it never gets

you anywhere.

Never in my life have I seen an Olympic runner don a heavy wool jacket to run a race. How ridiculous we must look to the Lord when we try to carry the baggage of doubt and anxiety with us. It is just not possible to keep our "pet sins" in the pockets of our jogging suits. No man can serve two masters (Matthew 6:24). Let's get rid of every weight. It will leave us with a sense of great satisfaction. Can you remember cleaning out the garage or a closet and the wonderful feeling of relief that you felt when all the junk was at last carted off? When pioneers traveled out west in their covered wagons, some of them started out with wagons stuffed full of furniture and other favorite belongings. But the weight became burdensome for the horses, and the heavy wagons were difficult to navigate over the rocks, creeks, and mud. Soon those prized items, though of great sentimental value, were tossed out in favor of practicality. It makes great sense to travel with only bare essentials in our suitcases. After all, when we get to heaven, we won't need luggage. We will be at home.

FOR DISCUSSION

1. What did Jesus tell the disciples to take with them on their journey? (Mark 6:8-9)

2. If you read Hebrews chapter 11, the "Hall of Fame of Faith" chapter and then Hebrews 12:1, do you think perhaps the greatest weight that one might cast off is doubt?

3. Did King Solomon ever repent of his idolatry or did he die in that state? (Ecclesiastes 12:13)

4. How might Solomon's 700 wives and 300 concubines have become a "weighty" sin for him?

MORE FUN THAN WEIGHTLIFTING

What weights did the following people cast off when they became Chritians?

- Paul (Acts 22:16): _____
  _____
  _____

- The Ethiopian Eunuch (Acts 8:30-39) :_____
  _____
  _____

- The Philippian Jailor (Acts 16:25-33): _____
  _____
  _____

- Believers in Jerusalem (Acts 2:41-47): _____
  _____
  _____

Chapter Twelve
If Ye Continue

While Jesus lived on this earth, the beloved apostle John appears to have been His best friend. John was in the inner circle of Christ's friends, along with Peter and James. You will find this group together at such events as the Transfiguration (Matthew 17:1-2; Mark 9:2-7; Luke 9:28-31) and at such places as the Garden of Gethsemane. (John 18:2) It was John who leaned on Jesus' bosom at the Last Supper. And at the foot of the cross, it was John to whom Jesus entrusted the care of His mother, Mary. That same John recorded these words of our Lord: *"If ye continue in My word, then ye are my disciples indeed; and ye shall know the truth, and the truth shall make you free"* (John 8:31b-32). This passage embodies the spirit of what I have been trying to say in this book: Walking in the light, being continually cleansed by the blood of Jesus Christ, and continuing in the word of Christ does make us free. This KNOWLEDGE of the TRUTH makes us CERTAIN OF OUR SALVATION!!!

God's word is so divinely correct that every part of it agrees perfectly with every other part. Continuing in the word of Christ, continuing in His goodness (Romans 11:22), continuing in the faith (Colossians 1:23), continuing in the things we have learned (2 Timothy 3:14), and continuing in the Son (1 John 2:24) is the same as walking in the light.

On the other hand, referring to the same scriptures in the previous paragraph, if we cease to walk in the light (1 John 1:7-8), if we cease to continue in His goodness, and fail to remain in the faith, we will be cut off from God, and we will fall from grace! Romans 6:1-2: *"What shall we say then? Shall we continue in sin that grace may abound? Certainly not! How shall we who died to sin live any longer in it?"*

At the risk of over-simplification, let me illustrate this principle with two examples: FEEDING A BABY: You can't just feed a baby his morning bottle and let him go at that! FUELING A CAR: You wouldn't just fill your gas tank once in New York and drive to Arizona. Do you get the point? You have to feed a baby morning, noon, night, and between meals. You have to re-fuel at intervals, or you will find yourself stranded. The spiritual application is that we must continue our walk with Christ, continue our daily prayers, continue to worship, and continue in fellowship with the saints. With this continued activity on our part, the blood of Jesus Christ will continue to cleanse us from all sin. *"For we are made partakers of Christ, if we hold the beginning of our confidence steadfast unto the end"* (Hebrews 3:14).

A little girl in elementary school had difficulty learning to spell. She lived with her grandmother, and the child's teacher gave the grandmother some helpful advice, instructing her to pour sand on the table and to let her granddaughter write her spelling words in the sand with her finger. The sense of touch reinforced the child's mental picture of what the words looked like. The teacher's advice worked! Just as we learn by both hearing and doing, the Bible plainly teaches that *"faith without works is dead"* and that *"by works a man is justified, and not by faith only"* (See James 2:24-26). It takes both.

The diagrams below are presented as a learning tool, but you must do what the concepts teach, or they are of no value to you whatsoever.

LEARNING TOOLS

The steps to salvation are out of order. Arrange them correctly by placing a number in the blank in the order in which they should be listed (1 for first, 2 for second, etc).

• Repentance (Acts 2:38) _____

• Hearing (Romans 10:13-17) _____

• Baptism (Acts 22:16) _____

• Confession (Romans 10: 9-10) _____

• Belief (Mark 16:16) _____

• Walking in the Light (1 John 1:7) _____

IT IS "NECESSARY" AND "REQUIRED" THAT WE BE "FAITHFUL."

- Revelations 2:10   Be thou faithful unto death.

- 2 Peter 2:20-22   overcome, entangled again

- Jude 1:21   Keep in God's love.

- Hebrews 3:12-14   Do not depart from God.

RESULTS:

- Matthew 25:21-23   Well done… faithful servant

- Revelations 2:10   Receive the crown of life

- Mark 8:34-37   Whosoever will come after me, let him deny himself, and take up his cross and follow Me. For whosoever will save his life, shall lose it; but whosoever shall lose his life for my sake and the Gospel's, the same shall save it. For what shall it profit a man, if he shall gain The whole world, and lose his own soul? Or what shall a man give in exchange for his soul?

Chapter Thirteen
When Time Shall Be No More

The eleventh chapter of Hebrews gives us a list and an account of the faithful Bible characters that make up the early patriarchs/matriarch. They include Abel, Enoch, Noah, Abraham, Sarah, Jacob, Isaac, Moses, and others who followed God and endured to the end.

"Wherefore seeing we also are compassed about with so great a cloud of witnesses, let us lay aside every weight, and the sin which doth so easily beset us, and let us run with patience the race that is set before us, Looking unto Jesus the author and finisher of our faith; who for the joy that was set before him endured the cross, despising the shame, and is set down at the right hand of the throne of God" (Hebrews 12:1-3).

Through the ages, children of God have followed God's commandments and have remained faithful to the end of their lives. And His faithful children will continue to swell the ranks of this great and marvelous number to be included on the "Day of Reckoning." We will stand before Christ on the Judgment Day, the day when the Lord shall return to gather His own and take us back to heaven with Him, where we will live eternally with God, Christ, and the Holy Spirit.

• *"And if children, then heirs; heirs of God, and joint-heirs with Christ; if so be that we suffer with him, that we may be also glorified together"* (Romans 8:16-17).

• 1 Corinthians 2:9 states: *"Eye hath not seen, nor ear heard, neither have entered into the heart of man, the things which God hath prepared for them that love Him."*

• 1 Corinthians 15:58 teaches us: *"Therefore, my beloved brethren, be ye steadfast, unmovable, always abounding in the work of the Lord, forasmuch as ye know that your labour is not in vain in the Lord."*

• In John 14:1-3, Jesus had just told His apostles of His upcoming betrayal and death on the cross. They were very upset, and Jesus said to them: *"Let not your heart be troubled, ye believe in God, believe also in Me. In My Father's house are many mansions, if it were not so I would have told you. I go to prepare a place for you and if I go and prepare a place for you, I will come again and receive you unto myself, that where I am there ye may be also."* Christ's words also apply to those of us who love God, who keep His commandments, and who are faithful to the end of their life.

• In Revelation 22:1-2, John wrote: *"And He shewed me a pure water of life, clear as crystal, proceeding out of the throne of God and of the Lamb. In the midst of the street of it and on either side of the river, was there the tree of life, which bare twelve manner of fruits, and yielded her fruit every month and the leaves of the tree were for the healing of the nations."*

Salvation is NOT A MATTER OF PERFECTION but is A MATTER OF BEING FAITHFUL UNTO DEATH (Revelation 2:10). Those who follow Christ faithfully can secure their salvation, including Christians who, though not perfect, just keep-on-keeping-on. The faithful have looked forward to seeing their Lord's face, receiving a "Rest," and joining all the saints who make up the tremendous group that will be given their reward, a "crown of life" and a "robe" (Revelation 2:10). They will be in a place where they will receive "eternal life" (Romans 6:23). What a grand and glorious day that will be!

As I conclude this book, it seems fitting that the last chapter should be about Heaven, our final resting place, and the place we yearn for. In heaven there will be no pain, no death (Revelation 21:4), no sorrow (Revelation 18:7), and no tears (Revelation 7:17). There will be no need for the sun and no need for the moon, because God's glory will be our light (Revelation 21:23). We will have one eternal day because there will be no night.

As this scene unfolds, our happiness and joy will be indescribable beyond measure. To see Jesus' face will be our greatest joy. Our faithfulness will have been worth all our persecutions and all our trials. Our tribulations will be as nothing when we view the streets of gold and the tree of life. 2 Corinthians 4:17 states: *"For our light affliction, which is but for a moment, worketh for us a far more exceeding and eternal weight of glory."* As we look over heaven's inhabitants, we will be filled with joy and happiness as we see our loved ones, our family, and our friends with us there. We are told that there will be no tears for those who are not there. God will not allow us

to be sad, He will wipe away our tears, and we will be comforted.
At last our long journey will be complete. What we have looked forward to for so long will become a reality. This day will be like no other! When Christ returns in a cloud, TIME WILL BE NO MORE. There will be no last minute appeals, no deathbed repentance, and no forgiveness. What a wonderful day for those who are ready and waiting for the Lord to return.

As you study this chapter and review the scriptures concerning the last day, we need to ponder the coming events, stay the course, run the race, and remain faithful to the end. Then we can look forward to the Lord's return when He will reward the faithful.

At last, I have found the answers I searched for so diligently. In my summation, let me share a few scriptures that are so encouraging to the child of God who desperately wants to avoid hell and gain eternal life in heaven when time is no more.

- There is no fear in love; but perfect love casteth out fear: because fear hath torment. He that feareth is not made perfect in love. We love him, because he first loved us. (1 John 4:18-19)

- *"O death, where is thy sting? O grave, where is thy victory?"* (1 Corinthians 15:55).

WHEN TIME SHALL BE NO MORE
(From King James Version)

EVENTS THAT WILL HAPPEN ON THAT DAY:

1. The _Lord_ _Himself_ shall _descend_ from _descend_ with a _shout_ (1 Thessalonians 4:16).

2. The Day of the _Lord_ will come as a _thief_ in the _night_ (2 Peter 3:10).

3. Every _knee_ shall _bow_ to me (Romans 14:11-12). +every tongue shall confess to God.

4. Christ will separate the _sheep_ from the _goats_ (Matthew

25:32-33).

5. Judgment must __begin__ at the __house__ of __God__ (1 Peter 4:17).

6. God has given to us __eternal__ __life__ (1 John 5:11). *This life is in His Son*

7. __Death__ and __Hades__ were cast into the __lake__ of __fire__ (Revelation 20:14). *This is second death.*

CHRIST'S MAJESTY, SACRIFICE, AND GLORY:

8. Though Christ was a __son__, yet learned he __obedience__ by the __things__ which he __suffered__. (Hebrews 5:8)

9. We have not a __high__ __priest__ which cannot be __touched__ *sympathy with our weakness* with the __feeling__ of our __infirmities__: but was in all points __tempted__ like as __we__ __are__. (Hebrews 4:15) *yet without sin*

DESCRIPTION OF HEAVEN:

10. The street of the city was __pure__ __gold__ (Revelation 21:21). *like transparent glass*

11. The city had no need of the __sun__ neither of the __moon__ (Revelation 21:23).

12. There shall be no __night__ there (Revelation 21:25).

WARNING TO HEED:

13. __Fear__ God and __keep__ His __commandments__, for this is the __whole__ __duty__ of man (Ecclesiastes 12:13). *man's all*

14. Be thou __faithful__ unto __death__, and I will give __you__ a __crown__ of __life__, (Revelation 2:10).

15. The __books__ were __opened__: and another __book__ was __opened__,

which is the _book_ of _life_ (Revelation 20:12). *and dead were judged according to their works*

16. The lessons from the parable of the ten virgins teach us that we must always be _ready_ (Matthew 25:1-10).

17. There remaineth therefore a _rest_ to the _people_ of God (Hebrews 4:9).

18. There shall be no more _death_, neither _sorrow_ nor _crying_, Neither shall there be any more _pain_ (Revelations 21:4). *For the former things are passed away*

19. For our _light affliction_, which is but for a _moment_, worketh for us a far more _exceeding_ and _eternal_ weight of _glory_ (2 Corinthians 4:17).

20. Blessed are they that _do His commandments_, that they may have _right_ to the tree of _life_, and may enter in through the _gates_ into the _city_ (Revelation 22:14). *Rev 22:15 But outside are the dogs, sorcerers & sexually immoral & murderers & idolaters & whoever loves & practices a lie*

21. And they shall see _His face_: and his _name_ shall be in their _foreheads_ (Revelations 22:4).

22. The _Spirit Himself_ itself beareth _witness_ with our _spirit_, that we are the _children_ of _God_ (Romans 8:16).

23. And there shall be no _night_ there; And they need no _lamp_, neither _light_ of the _sun_: for the Lord _God_ giveth them _light_; and they shall _reign_ for _ever_ and _ever_ (Revelation 22:5).

EVENTS TO OBSERVE CONCERNING THE LAST DAY:

- It will be unexpected.
- It will be an ordinary day when people will be marrying and given in marriage.
- God is the only one who knows that day.

- As we are found, so shall we be judged!!!
- The earth and all its elements shall be burned up with a fervent heat.
- There will be NO THOUSAND YEAR REIGN.
- Christ will not set up an earthly kingdom.
- The dead in Christ shall rise first, and those that remain alive will be changed in the twinkling of an eye, and they shall be caught up in the air to meet Christ.
- Christ is our savior now, but on that final day, he will be our judge.
- There will be NO MISTAKES with Christ's judgment.
- There will be no " appeals" or "second chances." Therefore it behooves us all to be ready for that great day when Christ will come back and judge every person who has ever lived.
- Christ will return the second time in a cloud, and he will not set foot on this earth.
- Christ will deliver his kingdom (church) to God (1 Corinthians 15:24).

DEEPER STUDY

Open your Bible and read the following scriptures for a "DEEPER STUDY" on the FINAL DAY. Circle the number of the scriptures you have read.

1. 1 Thessalonians 4:16
2. 1 Corinthians 15:52
3. 2 Peter 3:10
4. Romans 14:11
5. Matthew 25:32-33
6. 2 Timothy 4:1
7. 1 Peter 4:17
8. 1 John 5:11
9. Revelations 20:14-15
10. 1 Corinthians 15:55

SCRIPTURES ABOUT THE FINAL DAY

1. 1 Thessalonians 4:16: *"For the lord himself shall descend from heaven with a shout, and the voice of the archangel, and the trumpet of god; and the dead in Christ shall rise first."*

2. 2 Peter 3:10: *"But the day of the Lord will come as a thief in the night; in which the heavens shall pass away with a great noise, and the elements shall melt with a fervent heat, the earth also and the works that are therein shall be burned up."*

3. Romans 14:11: *"For it is written, every knee shall bow to me, and every tongue shall confess to God. So then every one of us shall give account of himself to God."*

4. Matthew 25: 32-33: *"And Christ shall set the sheep on his right hand, but the goats on the left. The King shall say to those on his right hand, "Come, inherit the kingdom prepared for you from foundation of the world."*

5. 2 Timothy 4:1: *"Jesus Christ shall judge the quick (living) and the dead at his appearing and his kingdom."*

6. 1 Peter 4:17: "Judgment must begin at the house of God, and if it first begins at us, what shall the end be of them that obey not the gospel of God?"

7. 1 John 5:11: *"And this is the record, that God hath given to us eternal life, and this life is in his Son."*

8. Revelations 20:14-15: *"And death and hell were cast into the lake on fire. And whosoever was not found written in the BOOK OF LIFE were cast into the lake of fire."*

9. 1 Corinthians 15:52: *"In a moment, in the twinkling of an eye, at the last trump: for the trumpet shall sound, and the dead shall be raised incorruptible, and we shall be changed."*

10. 1 Corinthians 15:55: " *'O death, where is thy sting? 'O grave, where is thy victory?"*

Appendix One
Pertinent Scriptures

GRACE

• *" For sin shall not have dominion over you; for ye are not under the Law , but under grace"* (Romans 6:14).

• *"That being justified by His grace, we should be made heirs according to the hope of eternal life"* (Titus 3:7).

• *"God resistheth the proud, but giveth grace to the humble"* (James 4:6).

• *"For the law was given by Moses, but grace and truth came by Jesus Christ"* (John 1:17).

• "And now brethren, I commend you to God and to the word of His grace, which is able to build you up, and to give you and inheritance among all them which are sanctified" (Acts 20:32).

• *"For the grace of God that bringeth salvation, hath appeared to all men"* (Titus 2:11).

SIN

• *" Know ye not that to whom ye yield yourselves servants to obey, his servants ye are to whom you obey; whether of sin unto death, or of obedience unto righteousness"* (Romans 6:16).

• *"Therefore to him that knoweth to do good, and doeth it not, to him it is sin"* (James 4:17).

• *"But god be thanked, that ye were the servants of sin, but ye have obeyed from the heart, that form of doctrine which was delivered you"* (Romans 6:17).

- *"Being then made free from sin, ye became the servants of righteousness"* (Romans 6:18).

- *"Be not overcome with evil, but overcome evil with good"* (Romans 12:21).

- *"In whom ye have redemption through His blood, the forgiveness of sins, according to the riches of His grace"* (Ephesians 1:7).

- *"The sting of death is sin"* (1 Corinthians 15:56).

- *"Draw nigh to God, cleanse your hands, ye sinners; and purify your hearts, ye double-minded"* (James 4:8).

LOVE

- *"In this was manifested the love of God toward us, because that God sent His only begotten son into the world, that we might live through Him"* (1 John 4:9-10).

- *"But as it is written, 'Eye hath not seen, nor ear heard, neither have entered into the heart of man the things which God hath prepared for them that love Him"* (1 Corinthians 2:9).

- *"Love your enemies, bless them that curse you, do good to them that hate you, and pray for them which, despitefully use you and persecute you"* (Matthew 5:44).

- *"Be kindly affectionate one to another with brotherly love; in honor preferring one another"* (Romans 12:10).

FEAR

- *"And fear not them which kill the body, but are not able to kill the soul; but rather fear Him which is able to destroy both soul and body in hell"* (Matthew 10:28).

- *"So that we may boldly say,' The Lord is my helper, and I will not fear what man shall do unto me"* (Hebrews 13:6).

- *"It is a fearful thing to fall into the hands of the living God"* (Hebrews 10:31).

- *"But the fearful, and the unbelieving, and the abominable, and murderers, and whoremongers, and sorcerers, and idolaters, and all liars, shall have their part in the lake which burneth with fire and brimstone: which is the second death"* (Revelation 21:8).

FAITH

- *"Therefore being justified by faith, we have peace with God through our Lord Jesus Christ: by whom also we have access by faith into this grace wherein we stand, and rejoice in the hope of the glory of God"* (Romans 5:1-2).

- *"For we walk by faith; not by sight"* (2 Corinthians 5:7).

- *"Even so faith, if it hath not works, is dead, being alone"* (James 2:17).

CONFIDENCE

- *"And this is the confidence that we have in Him, that, if we ask anything according to His will, He heareth us"* (1 John 5:14).

- *"And hope maketh not ashamed; because the love of God is shed abroad in our hearts by the Holy Spirit which is given unto us"* (Romans 5:5).

- *"Cast not away therefore your confidence, which hath great recompense of reward. For ye have need of patience, that, after ye have done the will of God, ye might receive the promise"* (Hebrews 10:35-36).

- *"In the fear of the Lord is strong confidence, and His children shall have a place of refuge"* (Proverbs 14:26).

- *"In whom we have boldness and access with confidence by the faith of Him"* (Ephesians 3:12).

- *"To the praise of the glory of his grace, wherein He hath made us accepted in the beloved"* (Ephesians 1:6).

• *"Knowing that of the Lord ye shall receive the reward of the inheritance: for ye serve the Lord Christ"* (Colossians 3:24).

• *"I can do all things through Christ who strengtheneth me"* (Philippians 4:13).

• *"Having therefore, brethren, boldness to enter into the holiest by the blood of Jesus"* (Hebrews 10:19).

MERCY

• *"But after that the kindness and love of God our Savior toward man appeared. Not by works of righteousness which we have done, but according to His mercy He saved us, by the washing and regeneration, and the renewing of the Holy Spirit"* (Titus 3: 4-5).

Appendix Two
Suggestions For Further Reading

Box, Charles. *"Bible Thoughts about Salvation."* The Reporter Greenville Alabama: Walnut Street Church of Christ, Vol 35, #17, April 26, 1996.

Cotham, Perry B. *"After Death...What then?"* (Sixth Edition). Grand Prairie, Texas: Perry B. Cotham. 1970.

Edwards, Earl D. *"Can A Christian Feel secure About His Salvation?"* The Restorer. March/April 1999.

Exum, Jack. *"How Do You Know That You Are Accepted....When You Fail And Do Not Do Good?"* Franklin Springs GA: Advocate Press.

Exum, Jack. *"Amazing Grace: God's Power to Be."* Lake City, FLA. (Third Printing) 2000.

Hutton, Vance. *"God Is So Good."* Bulletin Article in the Double Springs Informer. Double Springs, ALA: Double Springs Church of Christ. January 2006.

Kizer, Andy. *"The Providence of God Sermon Outline."* Haleyville, Alabama: 9th Ave. Church of Christ.

Wester, Stella G. *"The Hand of God Touched ...Me."* Abilene, TX Quality Publications, 1987.

Wilhelm, Jack *"A Study of God's People: Secure in Hope."* RSVP Newsletter, 1992.

Wilhelm, Jack. *"The Security of the Saints."* Sermon. Florence, Alabama.

Woodell, Jim. *"Are You Saved? Do You Know For Sure?"* (Tract) Condensed From *"Reaping With Romans- The Roman Approach."*

Woods, Guy N. Freed- Hardeman Lectureship Outline. *"How God Saves and Keeps Us,"* p 41. 1061.

Wyers, James F., minister of the Winfield Church of Christ, provided his outline for Open Bible Study.

Appendix Three
How God Saves and Keeps Us

INTRODUCTION:

1. Man is lost (Isaiah 59:1-2; Ephesians 2:1).
2. Salvation is possible (Romans 5:8).
3. A plan for continual cleansing from sin is available (1 John 1:7).

I. Need for plan for Christian as well as for alien sinner.
    A. Need for Plan because Christians sin also (1 John 1:8, 10).
    B. Passage affirming plan: 1 John 1:7-9.
        1. Analysis of plan:
            a. "If"- Condition.
            b. "We"-Christians (i.e., faithful ones).
            c. "Walk"-Greek literally means "keep on walking."
            d. "Light"-God's will or gospel.
            e. "Blood"-Cleansing agent.
            f. "Cleanseth"-Greek literally means "keeps on cleansing."
            g. "Sin"-object from which to be cleansed.

        2. Those contemplated-faithful Christians
            a. Revelation 2:10; Matthew 25:21, 23.
            b. Faithfulness vs. perfection.

II. Implications.
    A. Faithful are not under condemnation. Proved:
        1. Logically: if cleansed, then not condemned. Faithful are cleansed (cf. 1 John 1:7); therefore, not condemned.
        2. Authoritatively: Romans 8:1.
    B. Sin not imputed to the faithful. Proved:
        1. Logically: if not condemned, because:
            a. Never sins, or
            b. Sin not charged against him. 1 John 1:8, 10 reveals
        2. Authoritatively: Psalms 32:1, 2; Romans 4:8.

C. Windshield wiper illustration: Do not operate control each time windshield needs wiping, but set in motion a process that keeps on wiping the windshield. So it is with God's plan of constant cleansing of the faithful with Christ's blood.
D. Therefore, a constant sense of guilt or remorse is a reflection on God's grace.
E. Faithful Christians can and should live with assurance.

III. Objections considered.
    A. "Gives license to sin."
        1. No. Matter only concerned with the faithful.
        2. When we cease to do his will, God ceases to keep us clean. Lost!
    B. "Same as doctrine of impossibility of apostasy."
        1. No. If cease to be faithful, no longer covered by Christ's blood
        2. Not contending one cannot sin as a Christian.

IV. Applications.
    A. Assurance.
        1. If Christian sins ignorantly, he is not lost. (Example: No one knows all of God's will perfectly, so one may sin and never know it. If such person dies, is he lost or saved? Answer: if otherwise faithful, he is saved!)
        2. If a Christians sins through momentary weakness, he is not lost. (Example: Brethren quarrel. One loses control of tongue, leaves for home, and is killed in an accident. Is he lost or saved? If otherwise, faithful, he is saved)!
        3. If a Christian has a secret sin (i.e., those he has forgotten), he is not lost (Psalm 19:12). (Example: No one can remember everything he has done wrong. A Christian may sin and through faulty memory remember it. If he should die, would he be saved or lost? If otherwise faithful, he is saved)!
    B. Blessedness.
        1. Assurance of salvation (1 John 5:13).
        2. No fear of condemnation (Romans 8:1).
        3. Joy of living in hope (1 Thessalonians 4:13).
        4. A good conscience (Acts 23:1; 1 John 3:21)

V. Cautions.
    A. Overconfidence can lead to pride.
        1. Because these things are true does not mean that no dangers exist.
        2. 1 Corinthians 10:12
    B. Self-examination is needed.
        1. 2 Corinthians 13:5
        2. This keeps us sensitive to our need to walk faithfully in the light, covered by the cleansing power of Christ's blood.

Conclusion:

1. God's part of the plan involves cleansing us and keeping us cleansed, which he will do if we keep our part.

2. Our part of the plan is to be obedient and to remain faithful to God, with confidence in the assurance that he will continually cleanse us and have fellowship with us.

Outline adapted and arranged from How God Saves and Keeps Us: Basic Thoughts from Freed-Hardeman University Lectureship Outlines, 1961, *"How God Saves and Keeps Us,"* p. 41, Guy N. Woods. (Additional notes by James Wyers).

Appendix Four
Outline For Open Bible Study

A NOTE FROM THE AUTHOR:

During the early part of my journey when I was seeking answers about ***"Blessed Assurance,"*** a good friend and fellow Christian gave me a copy of An Outline for Open Bible Study. I got out my Bible and began diligently studying the scriptures contained in the outline. This study opened my eyes to many scriptures, and they taught me much of God's word. I have included this outline in my book because some of the readers might want to study this outline and share it with others.

I. It is impossible for God to lie (Hebrews 6:18-19).

II. God always keeps his promises (2 Peter 3:9).

III. The word thoroughly furnishes us (2 Timothy 3:16-17).

IV. We are saved by God's grace (through faith). We are not saved by our good works, our good morals, or our goodness, or because we deserve it ... for if this were the case, Christ's death would have been in vain.
- It is a paradox that good works will not save you, but you cannot go to heaven without good works.
- James 2:17 Even so faith, if it hath not works, is dead, being alone.
- James 2:26 For as the body without the spirit is dead, so faith without works is dead also.
- Ephesians 2:8-9 *"For by grace are ye saved through faith, and that not of yourselves; it is the gift of God; Not of works, lest any man should boast."*
- If we are giving a living sacrifice to God, we give our ALL, our Money, our efforts, our heart, and our influence. Within this frame work, God wants us to be busy people..."about my Father's business."

V. If we love Him, we will keep his commandments. *"If ye love me, keep my commandments"* (John 14:15).
"Let us hear the conclusion of the whole matter, Fear God, and keep his commandments, for this is the whole duty of man" (Ecclesiastes 12:13).

VI. Christ and God are jealous over us with a Godly jealousy.
"For I am jealous over you with godly jealous; for I have espoused you to one husband, that I may present you as a chaste virgin to Christ" (2 Corinthians 11:2).

VII. If we are His servants, we have assurance of salvation.
"And this is the confidence that we have in him, that, if we ask any thing according to his will, he heareth us. And if we know that he hear us, whatsoever we ask, we know that we have the petitions that we desired of him" (1 John 5:14-15).

VIII. The saved look forward to the Lord's coming. They watch and wait (1 Thessalonians 4:15-16).

Appendix Five

What Must I Do To Be Saved?
by Jerry Davidson

What must I do to be saved? This is the greatest, most important question that man has ever asked.

God doesn't want anyone to be lost. Consider the following scriptures:

• *"The Lord is not slack concerning his promise, as some men count slackness; but is longsuffering to us-ward, not willing that any should perish, but that all should come to repentance"* (2 Peter 3:9).

• *"Who will have all men to be saved, and to come unto the knowledge of the truth"* (1 Timothy 2:4)?

• *"For God so loved the world, that he gave his only begotten Son, that whosoever believeth in him should not perish, but have everlasting life"* (John 3:16).

• *"Jesus came from heaven to save the lost. For the Son of man is come to seek and to save that which was lost"* (Luke 19:10).

Jesus wants everyone in the world to hear about God's love and desire for them to be saved.
• 1st. Jesus commanded: *"Go ye therefore, and teach all nations, baptizing them in the name of the Father, and of the Son, and of the Holy Ghost: Teaching them to observe all things whatsoever I have commanded you: and, lo, I am with you always, even unto the end of the world. Amen"* (Matthew 28:19-20). Consider also Romans 10:13-15. Have you Heard the Gospel? The answer is either Yes or No. If the answer is Yes, then do you believe that it is true?

• 2nd. Jesus commanded: *"I said therefore unto you, that ye shall die in your sins: for if ye believe not that I am he, ye shall die in your sins"* (John 8:24). Consider the following passages: Hebrews 11:6; James 2:14-26;

Luke 6:46; Hebrews 5:8,9. Do you Believe the Gospel? The answer is either Yes or No. If the answer is Yes, then are you willing to Repent of your sins?

• 3rd. Jesus commanded: *"I tell you, Nay: but, except ye repent, ye shall all likewise perish"* (Luke 13:3). Consider also Acts 17:30-31 and Acts 2:38. Are you willing to Repent of your sins? Repentance is a change of mind that brings about a change of life. The answer is either Yes or No. If the answer is Yes, then are you willing to Confess your Faith in Christ as the Son of God?

• 4th. Jesus commanded: *"Whosoever therefore shall confess me before men, him will I confess also before my Father which is in heaven. But whosoever shall deny me before men, him will I also deny before my Father which is in heaven"* (Matthew 10:32-33). Consider also Romans 10:10 and Acts 8:36-37. Are you willing to Confess you Faith in Jesus as the Son of God? The answer is either Yes or No. If the answer is Yes, then are you willing to be Baptized into Christ?

• 5th. Jesus commanded: *"And he said unto them, Go ye into all the world, and preach the gospel to every creature. He that believeth and is baptized shall be saved; but he that believeth not shall be damned"* (Mark 16:15-16). Consider also Acts 22:16; 1 Peter 3:21; Galatians 3:27; Romans 6:3-4; Colossians 2:12. Are you willing to be Baptized into Christ? The answer is either Yes or No. If the answer is Yes, then why not do so NOW!

• 6th. Jesus commanded: *"…be thou faithful unto death, and I will give thee a crown of life"* (Revelation 2:10b).

I HOPE TO SEE YOU IN HEAVEN SOME SWEET DAY.

-Jerry Davidson

WHAT MUST I DO TO BE SAVED?

LOST

HEAR THE GOSPEL	BELIEVE THE GOSPEL	REPENT OF YOUR SINS	CONFESS YOUR FAITH	BE BAPTIZED INTO
Jesus said **MATT. 28:19-20**	**Jesus said** **JOHN 8:24**	**Jesus said** **LUKE 13:3**	**Jesus said** **MATTHEW 10:32**	**Jesus said** **MARK 16:15-16**
Romans 10:13-15	Hebrews 11:6 James 2:14-26 Luke 6:46 Hebrews 5:8-9	Acts 17:30-31 Acts 2:38 Matthew 21:28,29 Repentance is a change of mind.	Romans 10:10 Acts 8:36, 37 "I believe that Jesus Christ is the son of God."	Acts 22:16 1 Peter 3:21 Galatians 3:27 Romans 6:3-4 Colossians 2:12
STEP 1 YES / NO	STEP 2 YES / NO	STEP 3 YES / NO	STEP 4 YES / NO	STEP 5 YES / NO

S I N

SAVED

- CHRIST'S BODY, THE CHURCH
- ...SHALL BE SAVED.
- WASH AWAY THY SINS.
- ..DOTH ALSO SAVE US.
- ...BAPTIZED INTO CHRIST HAVE PUT ON CHRIST.
- RAISED TO WALK IN NEWNESS OF LIFE.
- BURIED WITH CHRIST BY BAPTISM.

Appendix Six
God's Master Plan for Salvation by Ruth Ann Howell

Let's compare the written Old Testament Covenant to the written New Testament Covenant that is first revealed in Acts 2 in the New Testament.

The Mosaic Covenant was a covenant of law to the Israelites through Moses. God expected Israel to accept and obey this covenant. It had many laws for the Jewish people to carry out, but it was impossible for them to do all of them. This made them feel guilty because they were unable to do all of them. The Israelites could not get forgiveness of sins under this covenant. Also, they could not have salvation through this covenant. The sacrifice for their sins was made by the blood of bulls and goats by the Levitical priests and the High Priest. The blood of bulls and goats could not take away the sins of the world. Their sins were rolled forward each year, and a "scape goat" was released into the wilderness to carry the sins forward for one year. (Hebrews 10:4 and Leviticus 16:10).

The Mosiac Covenant was only given to Israel. No other nation and no Gentiles were offered this covenant. This law was given for a particular people (Jews), and only given for a temporary period of time.

The Mosiac Covenant was not perfect, because if it had been perfect, there would not have been a need for a "New" and "Second Covenant." (Hebrews 8:6-8)

<u>It is interesting to notice why the New Covenant is so much better than the Mosiac Covenant.</u>

1. The gift of salvation was made possible for all men.

2. When Christ shed his precious blood on the cross, His blood could take away the sins of the world.

3. Christ made a once-and-for-all sacrifice for the sins of the world. He

would never have to go back and repeat this sacrifice again (Hebrews 10:12-14).

4. The blood of bulls and goats could not take away the sins of the world (Hebrews 9: 13-14).

5. God knew that mankind could not keep all the laws of the Mosiac Covenant, and he had always planned to establish a "new" and "Better Covenant" for all mankind.

6. The "New Covenant" would offer a plan in which mankind could obtain remission of sins (Acts 2).

Even before the "Foundation of the World, God had a plan that his Son, Jesus, would come to earth, to be born of a virgin, and that he would carry out God's mission on earth that He also planned for him to do. In God's master plan, he also planned that his New Testament Church would be established in Jerusalem on the Day of Pentecost (Chapter Acts 2:38).

Part of God's plan was that Christ would be crucified on the cross, he would taste of death, he would be buried, and he would rise from the dead. He would appear to the apostles and other witnesses (Acts 4:10). Then he would ascent to the Father in heaven on a cloud (John 14:1-3).

Also in God's plan, his Son would be the perfect sacrifice without spot or blemish, and he would die for the sins of the world (Ephesians 5:25-27).

In the fullness of time, this New Covenant would be given to all people and nations, and this would include the Gentiles. The mystery of the gospel would be revealed to the world when the apostle, Peter, preached the first gospel sermon as recorded in the chapter of Acts 2. This event was in Jerusalem on the Day of Pentecost in 33 A.D. The Church of Christ was established at this time. Peter revealed how a person could be saved. In Acts 2:38 Peter said, *"Repent, and be baptized every one of you in the name of Jesus Christ for the remission of sins, and ye shall receive the gift of the Holy Ghost."* Acts 2:47 states ...And the Lord added to the church daily such as should be saved."

In Hebrews 9:16 the scriptures explain that where a testament is, there must also be the death of the testator. The New Covenant in the New Testament couldn't go into effect until Christ died. Christ nailed the old Mosiac Law to the cross (Colossians 2:14).

Christ's written New Testament Covenant offered all nations (including Gentiles) the opportunity to have eternal salvation (forgiveness of sins) "in" Christ Jesus (2 Timothy 2:20).

The Mosiac Covenant was under law, and it offered no salvation. The New Covenant offers eternal salvation, and it is under grace. The Mosiac Covenant was based on works, and the New Covenant is based on faith and grace.

In the fullness of time, according to God's time-table, all of Jehovah's plans would come to pass.

We are a people that is so blessed to live under Christ's New Testament Covenant with better promises. We do not live by "works" as in the Mosiac Covenant, but we live by "faith" (Galations 3:11).

Also, the New Covenant is for all men, although the Old Covenant was for Israel only.

Activity: Please fill in the blanks in the following scriptures:

1. "But when the _____ of _____ was come, God sent forth his _____ , made of a _____, made under the _____" (Galatians 4:4).

2. "To redeem them that were _____ the _____, that we might _____ the _____ of _____:" (Galatians 4:5).

3. "Having made known unto us the _____ of his _____ _____ to his _____ pleasure in himself "(Ephesians 1:9).

4. "That in the _____ of the _____ of _____ he might _____ together in one all _____ in _____"

(Ephesians 1:10).

5. "For _____ so _____ the _____, that he gave his only _____ _____, that _____ believeth in _____ should not _____, but have _____ life" (John 3:16).

6. "Neither is there _____ in any other, for there is _____ other _____ under _____ given among _____ whereby we must be _____" (Acts 4:12).

7. "Jesus said to him, I am the _____, the _____, and the _____: no man cometh unto the _____ but by _____" (John 14:6).

8. Paul said, "For I am not _____ of the _____ of _____: for it is the _____ of _____ unto _____ to _____ _____ that _____, to the _____ first, and also to the _____" (Romans 1:16).

Appendix Seven
Poems by Kevin Patrick Dillon

I KNOW I'M SAVED

He called me through His Holy Word.
The sweetest story e'er I'd heard
Twas one of love from start to finish
No darkness could its lure diminish.

God sent His Son-a Holy Lamb
And now his precious child I am.
For I obey the Lord's command
To be baptized and now I stand.

Forgiv'n and cleansed from ev'ry sin.
My soul is pure and whole within.
Each day I walk within His light
His mercy steer my feet aright.

Someday I'll hear His voice invite
Me kindly to a mansion site.
Why beams a smile across my face?
Because I'm saved by His sweet grace!

Kevin Patrick Dillon, M.A.R.

FOR ONLY ONE

He left the ninety and the nine
In search of only one.
The other lambs were safe inside
The fold when day was done

"But this My sheep is Lost!" said He,
It's value is immense.
I'll whate'er it takes to put
This sheep back in My fence

The driving force that led His search
Was love for only one.
Although he loved the ninety-nine,
This last one must be won

He looked along the riverside
And in between the rocks,
And high and low in thickets dense
For tattered, woolly locks.

The tedious search led to the cross,
And with a final breath,
The Shepherd said, "Its finished!"
And hung His head in death.

But spying in the distance
The outline of the cross,
The lamb came to his Shepherd,
And he's no longer lost.

Kevin Patrick Dillon, M.A.R.

WE'RE STANDING AT THE JUDGEMENT

We're standing at the judgment
My bosom friend and I,
We're smiling at each other,
Our joy we can't deny

Our lives were hard as Christians.
We suffered through some straits.
But all of this was worth it.
Now joy is on our plates.

You shared the gospel with me.
You told me"bout the Lord."
And now we're standing at His throne
To get a great reward.
We're standing at the judgment
My bosom friend and I
Behind us are a lot of friends
Who never more will die'
For they have life eternal.

We taught to them the way
That led them straight to Jesus
And they rejoice today

When you stand at the judgment,
You also will rejoice
If all those standing 'round you
Heard Jesus through your voice.

Kevin Patrick Dillon, M.A.R.

ACKNOWLEDGEMENTS:

Our sincere gratitude to James F. Wyres, minister of the Winfield Church of Christ, who provided his outline for our use and gave us valuable comments via phone conversation on March 27, 2006.

I owe a debt of gratitude to Kevin Dillon, my brother in Christ. Without his help, encouragement, and his prodding me; this book would never have become a reality. Thank you Kevin.

My sister in Christ, Donna Reedy, has been a good friend and encouragement to me as I worked on the manuscript for this book. She has made suggestions, re-typed notes and wiped away all my tears as we discussed the need for this material to be made available for both Christians and those who are lost and in need of someone to teach them the amazing gospel of Christ.

I want to give a special thank you to Bonnie Alvis, Crystal Schieber, Andrew Schieber, and Paula Dill, for encouraging me to get the book finished, and published.

BIOGRAPHY

Ruth Ann Howell was born to L.C. Fuller, Jr. and Helen (Granade) Fuller in Russellville, Alabama, on October 4, 1940. She and David Howell were married on May 29, 1959. Until June 2004, they lived in Haleyville, Alabama. Currently, they live in Orange Beach, Alabama. They have two children, six grandchildren, and two great-grandchildren.

Ruth Ann's husband, David, preached at the Barn Creek Church of Christ for nine years, at the Burleson Church of Christ for 20 years where he also served as an elder, and at the Spruce Pine Church of Christ for four years. He has served as a trustee for Faulkner University in Montgomery, Alabama, for over 40 years. Currently, David serves as a deacon at the Summerdale Church of Christ in Summerdale, Alabama, and works with the *'Getting to Know Your Bible'* television program. David is a real estate agent on the Gulf Coast.

Across the years, Ruth Ann has been an active and supportive preacher's wife and an elder's wife for her husband, and she has been active in community and church work. Ruth Ann has spoken at various lectureships and ladies days, and has taught children's and ladies' bible classes for many years. She has been very successful in one-on-one Bible studies with ladies.

Concerned with the salvation of the lost, Ruth Ann has been active in classes to teach other women how to conduct personal Bible studies. Her book, *'Blessed Assurance: Hope an Anchor of the Soul'* (Hebrews 6:19) encourages readers to become and to remain God's children, teaches them how to study the scriptures, and encourages Christians to never lose hope but to reach for the "High Calling of God" so they can spend eternity in heaven.

Billy Lambert, minister of the Summerdale Church of Christ and speaker for the *'Getting to Know Your Bible'* television program states: "Ruth Ann is a member of the Summerdale congregation. She has conducted women's classes on personal evangelism, and souls have been saved as a result. While she is concerned for the salvation of others, she has struggled with her own assurance. Finding her assurance has been a journey of many years, but she is finally at peace. Ruth Ann wants to share her peace with others, and she has laid out the road that leads to that blessing.